ISLAM
AND THE PROBLEM OF
ISRAEL

Ismail Raji Al- Faruqi

Qadeem Press

Qadeem Press

Qadeem Press Edition
Breathing Life into Forgotten Pages
www.qadeempress.com

Reprinted by Qadeem Press in 2025

Contents

Chapter I:
The Three-Cornered Nature of the Problem

A. Historical Preview

The problem of Israel confronting the Muslim World today has neither precedent nor parallel in Islamic history. The Muslim World has tended to regard it as another instance of Modern colonialism, or at best, as a repetition of the Crusades. The difference is not that Israel is neither one of these; but that it is both and more, much more. Unfortunately, there is no Islamic literature on the subject. The need for this analysis of the problem is, therefore, as great as the present moment which calls upon the Arab World in particular and the Muslim World in general to accept Israel as an integral member of a world-of- Muslim-nations in Asia-Africa.

The "Problem of Israel" is a three-cornered affair, involving the Muslim World, Western Christendom, and the Jews. The first two have been locked in struggle ever since the rise of the Islamic state in Madinah in 622. Indeed, even earlier. Christian commercial interest had pushed Abyssinia into launching a colonialist venture in South Arabia in 560 A.C. and an attempt to destroy the power of Makkah in the "Year of the Elephant," or 570 A.C., the year of the birth of the Prophet Muhammad (*salla Allahu 'alayhi wa sallam*). Even as early as that time, Western Christendom saw fit to use the religious zeal of Eastern Christians in order to exploit both them and the pre-Islamic Arabs for commercial profit. Pre-Islamic Arabia was a religious vacuum at the time, and the Christians of the West who held the reins of power in their hand were not concerned with preaching the faith. Rather, they were immersed in political struggles on the internal front, and economic and military struggle on the external. Arabia had no significance for them except as a trade route. When the new Islamic state began to raise its head following the integration of Makkah and most of the tribes of Western and South Arabia, Byzantium saw fit to mobilize its puppet armies in South Palestine and Jordan, a move which brought about the first military encounter between Islām and Christendom, the Campaign of Mu'tah (9 A.H./631 A.C.).

Previously, the Qur'anic revelation had said what it had to say concerning Christian doctrine, and through the personal conduct of the Prophet (SAAW), the Islamic state had laid down what her relation to Christians would be. The delegation from Christian Najran was well received by the Prophet (SAAW) and given full honour and hospitality. They were presented with Islam. Some accepted it and henceforth became integral members of the Muslim ummah. Others rejected it, and their decision was respected. They accepted the Pax Islamica and became an autonomous community endowed with its own law and institutions, its own destiny and momentum - an integral part of the universal Islamic state. But Christendom to the north could not countenance such arrangement. That is why when the Prophet (SAAW) sent two companions to Dhat al Talh to preach Islām, they were beheaded, and the confrontation became imminent.

From that time on, the relation between the Islamic state (then till now the Muslim World) and Christendom has been one of confrontation. Periods of relative inactivity on their common frontiers there certainly were. But these were temporary respites, due to the exhaustion of the two parties. In vain did the Muslim World offer Christendom the Pax Islāmica dictated by the Islamic state's constitution. Behind the still lines, stood a Christendom frustrated by its temporary inability to subdue the Muslim World.

No sooner had Christendom re- covered strength than it directed its fury and expansion in the direction of the Muslim World: against the Muslim petty states in Spain, the Ottoman caliphate in East Europe, the Muslims in West Africa, the Indian Ocean, the Malay Basin. The result was colonialism. The Muslim World has seen every kind of it: The European settler type - in Algeria; the intrusion of alien non-Muslim elements into Muslim societies - in Malaysia, Indonesia, Cyprus, Palestine; and economic exploitation, cultural imperialism, church mission, prevention of awakening and growth, spreading discord and fitnah (subversion) - everywhere. When the Muslim World arose in armed resistance to this alien and alienating presence in its midst, Christendom only changed its tactics and quickly adapted its means to the new situation. Military occupation and colonial administrations were terminated; but colonialism continued in subtle yet more devastating ways.

The downfall of the Ottoman Empire was received in the Christian West with great jubilation because it marked the end of Muslim hegemony in the world, even in the territory of Islām itself. The peoples of Islam were now to be subject to Christian Western dominion; and their Islamic identity, unity, culture as well as religion must now be confounded and shattered. Only thus may the general resentment and hatred inherent in the heart of the Christian West be satisfied.

B. Western Interest and the Near East

The problem of Israel is inextricably linked to this fourteen-centuries-old struggle between the Muslim World and Christendom. When Balfour made his nefarious declaration in 1918, he was continuing an old tradition which sought to rule by dividing the ruled, and to implant in the area a foreign body doomed to remain at odds with the rest - in short, to apply the principle of divide et impero. When the route to India and the Far East went around Africa, colonies at the Cape of Good Hope, the East coast of Africa, Aden, the littoral of the Arabian Peninsula, were necessary to safeguard that route. Opening of the Suez Canal made it necessary for Britain to occupy Egypt, to plan to neutralise Arabia and wrest the Eastern coast of the Mediterranean (Palestine, Jordan, Syria, Lebanon) from Muslim (Ottoman) control.

These territories were also valuable for their own sake. The Nile Valley produced sugar and rice for the world markets and the finest cotton in the world for the English textile mills. The Eastern Mediterranean lands produced wheat and fruits close enough to be transported to Europe in ships before the days of refrigeration. Plans for the production of 'Iraqi and Irānī oil were conceived prior to World War I and were put into effect as soon as the occupation of the territories was complete. On top of all these, the strategic military value of these territories for the empires of Britain, France, Italy, and Holland surpassed all considerations.

Two overriding American interests dictated assumption by the United States of the whole burden of European colonialism in the area following World War II: Anti-U.S.S.R. military strategy and oil. The creation of the state of Israel served at once all the following purposes: First, to provide, in case of another world war, a friendly base whose friendship to the West depends upon its own inevitable need for protection by the West for survival; Second, to provide a sore capable of draining all energies and resources of the surrounding areas so as to retard, if not to render impossible, any national reconstruction that would make them more capable of resisting Christian Western domination; Third, now that oil has been discovered in the Arabian Peninsula in the thirties, to provide a strong but dependent friendly Israel which can be counted upon to assist in the securing of this tremendous and vital resource; Fourth, to provide a cause which would throw the whole area into constant turmoil and thus enable Western dominion to fulfil its colonialist exploitative objectives more cheaply and easily; Fifth, to provide an apparently non-Western "hatchet" which can be manipulated and hurled by the West at any state seeking to rid the area of Christian Western influence; Sixth, to provide relief to the Christian Western conscience ridden with the guilt-complex of Christendom's crimes against the Jews over two millennia culminating in Hitler's holocaust; Seventh, to subvert the worldly power of the religion of Islām by splitting the ummah (its world community) into an Asian half and an African half separated by an insurmountable barrier.

C. Zionism and Western Goals

All these goals are consistent with the general will of the Christian West, locked as it saw and deemed itself to be, into a life and death struggle with Islām. If there was never any Jewish problem in the West, if there never was any Zionism, the Christian West would have created one. Indeed, they did create many other "Israels" in the Muslim World. They planted the Chinese in Malaya and created the State of Singapore; they planted the Greeks in Cyprus, Greeks and Italians in Alexandria, Armenians in Lebanon, and deliberately created so many more potential "Israels." The typology of the Christian West's action vis-à-vis the Muslim World has always been the same. Wherever they had the power, they so rearranged the boundaries of the Muslim territories under their dominion so as to include within each an alien element that promised to remain at odds with the Muslim community and thus constitute a permanent impediment to its liberation and progress.

All this and much more every Muslim child knows. This essay does not have for purpose to repeat it. Rather, what is sought here is to emphasise the point that the Christian- Muslim confrontation was raised to new heights of danger, of ferocity and bitterness when the Christian West discovered Zionism as a willing instrument of its anti-Muslim World hostility. That is the significance of the Balfour Declaration for Christian-Muslim-Jewish relations. America made this discovery only during World War II, and gave it official endorsement when Truman put the United States squarely behind the Zionist movement by asking Britain to open Palestine for unrestricted Jewish immigration in 1945.

*** *** ***

What is the nature of Zionism? What is its history? What is the internal force which has kept it alive? What is the nature of its appeal to the mind of the Western Jew? of the Western Chris- tian? If Judaism is old, and Zionism very new, how do they differ and what is their relation to each other? Why did Zionism insist on having a state - Israel? Why did the State of Israel behave as it did towards its neighbours? Must Israel always remain a Zionist state? How does the advent of the State of Israel look from the standpoint of Islam? How is the ideological war between Israel and the Muslim World to be treated? What is Islam's verdict today concerning Israel? May it be recognised under the terms of the shari'ah? What changes or conditions need to be instituted in order to make such recognition legitimate? Is the secular Palestinian state the Islamic answer to the problem of Israel? Suppose the whole machinery of the State of Israel were dismantled, what would Islām replace it with? How would Islamic constitutional law, under the circumstances, regulate future Muslim-Jewish relations? These and other questions are the subject of the present work.

Chapter II:
Aperçu of Jewish History in the Christian West Prior to the Emancipation

The Christians understood, or misunderstood, the career of Jesus as one of a god sent down to earth to suffer the most ignominious death as an atonement and oblation for the sins of man. In consequence, they reinterpreted the whole history of the Jews as a propadeutic for this great event. If there is to be a crucifixion of a god, there had to be a historical situation in which a saviour-God could be expected, accused to be the false saviour, and then crucified. There had to be a religion, Judaism, which develops so as to reach the fossilized state of literal legalism, in which rabbis had plunged their faith in the "fullness of time," and into the context of which the god to be crucified could enact his reform and be prosecuted and condemned in the process. The whole of the Jewish past and present was reduced to the status of an instrument, complex and winding, but still an instrument, for the incarnation and crucifixion of Jesus.

The Christians did not, in the main, reject or chastise the Jews on account of that pre-crucifixion history. On the contrary, they adopted it wholesale as their own and, through eisegesis, interpreted it as the gradual unfolding of the divine purpose in history. This adoption however broke down at the very crux of that history. The vilification, calumniation, false accusation, condemnation and crucifixion of Jesus, the Chris- tians could not perceive as steps necessary for consummation of the divine drama. Their conscience could not absolve the Jews for their active instrumentality in these events. Instead of thanking them for their role, as the logic of their claim would require, they indicted them with the supreme sin, that of deicide. As they remembered the passion of Jesus at every Easter - indeed at every mass and communion, at the mere sight of the ubiquitous crucifixes which stood ever-ready to remind them of the death of their saviour-God - their hearts seethed with hatred and resentment for the Jews as evil perpetrators of deicide.

Had the Jews all converted to Christianity, the Christian conscience would have been satisfied to ascribe deicide to a people that once was. The Christians would have vented their vengeance and resentment against beings present only in their imagination. But as it turned out, the Jews continued to exist, to reject the Christians' claim concerning Jesus-nay, to denounce Jesus as an impostor. Obviously, their existence as Jews was a blaring challenge to the Christian claim that Jesus was the Messiah and God. Their survival was for the Christians a constant and living reminder of the passion of Christ.

Two more elements pressured the Christian mind to jump from the living Jewish presence as a reminder of Christ's passion, to indicting that presence as itself guilty of that hideous crime. The first was supplied by scripture which reported that the prosecutors of Jesus acknowledged the indictment of Jesus as their deliberate work and accepted responsibility for it (Matthew 27:1, 12, 20, 22). It reported them as willing and ready to assume that responsibility then, in their own persons, as well as on behalf of all their future generations (Matthew 27:25). The Jews may deny that they have ever rendered such confession. Since the source is Christian, another prior element in the Christian mind must have made such futuristic indictment possible. That is the Christian doctrine of vicariousness of guilt, of suffering and of merit. Vicariousness is absolutely essential to the Christian faith. First, the sin of Adam, it is claimed, has passed to all his descendants and his guilt has vicariously become theirs, in the flesh. All men are necessarily and universally sinful, fallen and guilty; and no effort or moral striving on their part will ever save any of them. Original sin, Christianity holds, is in the flesh, innate and in- evitable. Because it is so, it took God Himself to pull man out of his predicament of doom. That is why God had to send His only son to ransom man from this necessary despair. Ta'ālā Allahu 'ammā yaşifun (Glorified be Allah above their descriptions of Him)!

Secondly, the suffering of Jesus is vicarious too. As agony and merit, it too passes mysteriously from Jesus to all men. Because Jesus died on the cross, so their argument claims, this or that Christian man living two thousand years later is personally deserving of Jesus' merit; for that merit has passed vicariously to him. It took a mind governed by such category of vicariousness on the moral level to jump to the conclusion that the contemporary Jewish neighbour is personally guilty of deicide, of rejection of Christ, of continuing "perfidy," as the contemporary Christian is personally saved, because he has personally deserved the merit Jesus had incurred in his atonement.

Indeed, it was the Pope himself who assumed official responsibility for protecting the Jew as a specie of satanic-ness, a living example of perfidy and unfaith, an archetype of the deicidal crime, as an antichrist. He established a special quarter for the Jews in Rome as a kind of horror museum in which to keep and show off these specimens of ungodliness for the enlightenment and education of the Christian community.

The list of social, legal and religious incapacities of the Jews of Christian Europe was long, and practically every Christian monarch added to it. Its highlights are that the Jews may not employ Christians, own Christian slaves, disinherit their children who convert to Christianity; that they must convert to Christianity if they marry a Christian; that they shall be ruled by Roman law rather than Torahic law; that they shall not criticise Christian doctrine nor give evidence against Christians; that they shall not celebrate Jewish feasts, practice circumcision, refrain from eating pork; that they must submit to baptism and refrain from reading the Torah in Hebrew or listening to its interpretation by their rabbis; that Jews shall refrain from practicing their customs, from preparing unleavened bread; that they be punished if they work on Sunday and not on Saturday; that they should marry according to Christian custom; that their children be brought up by Christian teachers; that Jews must pay special taxes, not appear in public between Holy Thursday and Easter, not hold any public office, not practice medicine on the Christians, etc. etc. Justinian ordered all Jews to be forced to listen to Christian teaching, their synagogues destroyed, and he prohibited them to read the Mishnah. Indeed, he prohibited the Jew under penalty of death "to raise his impious voice to contradict the evident purpose of God the resurrection the judgment... the work of God" (E. A. Synan, *The Popes, and the Jews in the Middle Ages.* New York, Macmillan, 1965, p. 17ff).

The Jews lived under such conditions in Europe for nearly two millennia. Often, they were banished from their cities for no crime other than being Jewish or for practicing Judaism. Following the Inquisition in Spain and Portugal, they were forcefully evicted from those countries or baptized and counted as Christians. They were also evicted from Britain and were not readmitted until Oliver

Cromwell, though with great restrictions to their civil rights. When the Crusades were launched, the Christian armies fell upon the Jewish population of every Christian city on their way, robbing, terrorizing, and slaughtering them as helpless prey while the monarchs and lords of the land looked on.

Naturally, there was no one to receive them except the Muslim World. The Jews of Spain poured into North Africa where they found their fellow Jews free and prospering. They were admitted on equal par with the Muslims banished from Spain. Muslim countries from Morocco to Egypt did their utmost to welcome and rehabilitate these refugees from Christendom. To this day there are whole villages in North Africa composed of the descendants of these refugees, Muslim and Jewish.

Under such limitations, it was natural that the Jews of Europe would at least live together in the same quarter to provide themselves with a measure of security. Since they were prohibited to employ Christians, agriculture was impossible for them; and so was public office. They had to make a living in trade and moneylending and, where possible, in medicine, pharmacy, astronomy and "magic." Individually, the Jew was an outlaw whenever he ventured outside of his ghetto. He was an un-citizen because the king or government of the land never recognized him as individual. Only as a member of his ghetto community did he exist legally, or did he pay any taxes. To an ignorant and superstitious people as the Europeans were in Middle Ages, the Jew's medical practice, astronomy and other sciences which they preserved from antiquity or learned from the Muslims, were regarded by the Christians as "black magic." Their money-lending operation was abominable usury. Since the ghetto could not grow in area, the natural increase of population aggravated the health hazards and made the situation still more repulsing. Extortion, secret dealings, blackmail, pawn brokerage and moneylending, persecutive and repressive measures which could be lifted only through bribery, blackmail, or prostitution, made the quality of human life in the ghetto sordid and ugly.

The religious base of this Christian hatred was only to be reinforced by the Jews' success as pawnbrokers, traders, and moneylenders. The Jews quickly became the moneyed middle class of Christian cities, living parasitically on the production or consumption of Christians. Naturally, their wealth was envied, often forcefully confiscated, but they managed on the whole to emerge from every crisis stronger and richer. Many a pope and many a prince dealt with them, borrowed their money, used their trade connections, or benefited from their medical knowledge. The Jew's contacts with the gentiles increased noticeably as the cities grew and trade and communications developed. As early as the Renaissance, these contacts with Christians were to influence and help Europeanise the Jews, as the diaries and letters of Rabbi Leon da Modena testify. However, many Jews could not resist the temptation to migrate to the Muslim World if migration were at all possible. More often the only way out of their misery was conversion to the faith of their enemies.

Those that resisted the temptation to convert and persisted in their Judaism, became still more attached to their faith and to one another in the process. From their terrible fate, the Jews derived a great advantage, namely, increase in communal awareness which diaspora conditions had first nearly dissipated. Christian persecution, denial of civil rights and incarceration within the bounds of the ghettos, could not but help reinforce the Jews' ethnic solidarity. The local governments did not deal with the Jews singly, as legal persons, but collectively. In consequence, Jewish rabbis acquired increased authority, and set up among themselves the essential rudiments of a ghetto government, of public and social services. Thus, a sort of "state within the state" gradually emerged, the former assuming responsibility for enforcement of Jewish law and representation of Jews before the officials of the latter. Taxes were imposed upon the Jews as a collective and the rabbis took upon themselves to portion out the levy among individuals. This arrangement consolidated and buttressed their authority and disciplined the individual Jew into communal loyalty. Outside the collective, the individual Jew was by and large an outlaw whom any powerful Christian could legitimately overcome, kill, or dispossess of his property. Any false accusation of blasphemy or of merely following a Jewish custom could only bring up the Christian neighbourhood or countryside against him.

Envy for the Jews' accumulated wealth, or for his secret wisdom and knowledge, was not only common, but the rule. However, it may have contributed to the Christian's hatred for and persecution of the Jews, it cannot serve as explanation of the Western phenomenon of anti-Semitism. Religious hatred is certainly prior and it, rather than envy, is the source which constantly replenished the Christians' resentment. What the Christians took to be ultimate reality or God was not only denied but declared an "impostor." What they regarded as summum bonum or salvation was scoffed at as hallucination. The ignominious crucifixion of their "God" was declared fully de- served by a pretender who denied the holiness of "the Law." Moreover, the Christians had a mind bent on sacramentalism and vicariousness, naive enough to believe the Church's claims for ontological passage of guilt, suffering and merit. It would seem as if all the ingredients were there to produce the most violent religious hatred; for Christian consciousness to vent itself against the only helpless scapegoat in their midst.

Chapter III:
The Emancipation and Its Aftermath

A. Revelation vs. Reason

The revelation which came to Muhammad (SAAW) summoned reason to prove the thesis of Islam. It never asserted its truths in defiance of reason, nor did it ever seek to overwhelm the noetic function of the mind. On the contrary, it always sought to convince its audience in harmony and unity with reason. When the Mu'tazilah sought to give reason an edge over revelation, or the Murji'ah to give revelation an edge over reason, the Muslim mind demurred and held its original position tenaciously, namely, that no contradiction between reason and revelation is final, that no disparity between them is beyond overarching and composition by reconsidering the meanings of revelation which might have been misunderstood, or the conclusions of reason which might have gone astray. From al Ma'mün to al Mutawakkil (197-232 A.H./813 847 A.C.), the three decades of Mu'tazilah ascendency, the problem acquired crisis proportions and was then solved forever.

Unlike Islām, Christianity was deeply committed to one side. Jesus' cool argumentation with his disciples quickly gave way to Paul's outcry that Athens had nothing to do with Jerusalem. "The Greeks seek after wisdom. But we teach Christ crucified unto the Jews a scandalon and unto the Greeks foolishness... God has chosen the foolish things of the world to confound the wise;... the weak... the base... despised things... things which are not to bring to nought the things which are" (I Corinthians, 1). Islam's rational wind had to blow on Christian Europe a long time before it awakened her gradually from her dogmatic slumber. Thomas of Aquinas had to be excommunicated for his rationalist "Averroism" before he regained acceptance; and Bruno, Galileo and countless others had to suffer persecution or death for daring to oppose reason to revelation. In Islām, revelation stood alone and had no institution divinely appointed to guard it. It had to speak for itself, to convince its audience and safeguard its truth by its sheer power to win the assent of the free mind. In Christianity, the Church was the guardian of its revelation by divine appointment, and it fought ferociously to save its domain against attack by reason and its stepdaughter, natural science. However detracted or resisted, the forces of reason gradually won. The magisterium of the Church was slowly but surely ignored, and her prestige in the circles of learning and science suffered terrible blows, as any history of science in the West would show.

B. The Enlightenment

The Enlightenment, which animated intellectual life in the seventeenth and eighteenth centuries, served as basis for much of science and culture in the West. It was a movement which adopted the standpoint of reason in reordering the worldview of Christian man. Priority was taken away from faith and the Church and restored to reason. Reason was declared a public prerogative of everyone who cared to cultivate it. No one could be excommunicated from its realm. It could not be combated by authority, but by itself and under its own rules. Its cultivation and use became the criteria of truth, of virtue and merit, not one's affiliation to the Church. Human beings came to be recognised as rational by nature; and it is this nature, rather than revelation or the teaching of the Church, that became the basis of human association, of government and social order. "Religious tutelage," the most degrading of all, as Kant had called it, was replaced by a new freedom in which rules were self-imposed and where all men - Jews included - were recognised as possessing an innate right to participate. Overnight, the Jews who had hitherto existed on sufferance, as aliens in the land, became equal citizens of a universal community of humans based on their participation in the realm of reason.

Their actual enfranchisement however had to await the political reconstitution of Europe.

C. Emancipation, at Last!

This did not tarry. France, where the new rationalist spirit had been fermenting since and even before Descartes, burst into the new era under the war cry of the Revolution: Liberté! Egalité! Fraternité! It exported the new ideology to Europe as its revolutionary (later, imperial) army swept away one European monarchy after another. As French soldiers entered a city, the walls of its Jewish ghetto came tumbling down. The Jews emerged as equal citizens of the new regime everywhere. Laying aside all their legal and social incapacities, the Jews of Europe plunged headlong into the new paradise whose gates were now flung wide open before them. It was a genuine "emancipation."

As they entered into their new lives, they first had to learn the vernacular language of the land. This they did with such vehemence that in one generation their masses in Central and Western Europe forgot Hebrew or Yiddish, their own ghetto language, and appropriated the vernacular languages of Europe as their own. Their sons could now enter the universities, join the national army, or serve in public office. Every section of society was now open to them. Their previous inexperience in agriculture prompted them to live in the cities, and to invest their efforts in industry, trade, finance, the professions, communications, and city development. Their social recovery was amazingly strong and swift. By 1797, they began to find their place even in the elected legislative bodies of Europe. Rather than a tolerated stranger, the Jew found himself perfectly at home in the expanding, industrialising, nation-states of Europe. His religious difference from the rest lost its importance in the new wave of secularism in all matters. In traditional normative Christian doctrine, no relevance of religion to civic life was claimed. This was the "realm of Caesar." If in actual practice this was not the case, and the Church did interfere and oft dominated, its power had been shaken by the Reformation and completely swept away by the nationalising British monarchy, the rationalising Enlightenment, and finally, the secularising French Revolution. Now, reason alone hence national utilitarianism - in which all men participate in degrees independently of their religious affiliation, was declared the basis of all civic decisions. Therefore, it was reasoned, the Jew may freely join in the new life of Europe on equal par with the Christian.

D. Assimilation and Reform

The greatest advocate of Jewish assimilation in Europe was Moses Mendelssohn, who lived before the French Revolution and helped to spread the "Enlightenment" mentality in Germany. He translated the Talmud into German for the double purpose of acquainting the Germans with Judaism, and the Jews who had already forgotten Hebrew, with their own faith. His classic counsel to his fellow Jews was to Germanise themselves in every respect and remain loyal to the Jewish faith which he conceived as something applicable to the religious sphere, a realm reduced to the internal relation of self to God, not unlike Christianity. However, Mendelssohn insisted that whereas Judaism is not a creed - the mind of a Jew being free to accept any conclusion of reason the Jew ought to follow Jewish law. This was easier said than done. Mendelssohn founded a periodical in Hebrew to bring assimilation and the new culture to the conservatives who still lingered and hesitated.

How to apply Jewish law to the external deed and, at the same time, to observe European custom and social ethic was never solved. The Europeans, for their part, expected the Jews to obliterate all that distinguished them from Christians. When the Jews resisted, the Christians compelled them to do so, no more in the name of religion, but in that of nationalism and national culture. Even their names, the Jews had to change or have them arbitrarily changed for them.

Assimilation generated its own momentum. The Jews' exposure to the cultural and religious life of Europe produced in them an inferiority complex towards their Christian neighbours, which they began to emulate even in the religious field. This emulation is the foundation of Reform Judaism, a new sect whose very name is indicative of the Christianised Jewish outlook. "Reform" has changed the liturgy, legitimised liturgical use of the vernacular languages instead of Hebrew, eliminated the long recitation of piyyutim and Torah, introduced the choir and playing of musical instruments in the synagogues. Some of these reforms were introduced into the Adat Jeshurun Synagogue in Amsterdam in 1796, and they were adopted in toto by the synagogues of Seesen in 1810, and of Hamburg in 1818. Slowly but surely, the new "Reform" spread to most other synagogues of Western Europe.

Emancipation and its consequence, assimilation, continued to produce problems for Judaism. Above all, it exposed Judaism to the same rending strains to which Christianity was already exposed, especially, Biblical criticism. Detached, objective examination of scripture had previously exploded the claim that the Pentateuch was the writing of Moses, or that any part of the Hebrew scripture was revealed by God verbatim. Historical textual analysis had established that the scripture had come from widely different traditions and disparate periods of time. It uncovered many discrepancies and mistakes in the Biblical text. All of this had forced the Christians to alter their theory of revelation. Partly, they recoursed to allegorical interpretation to fit the text into Christian doctrine; and partly, since the whole of Jewish history was for them a propaedeutic to the incarnation, they began to regard the scripture as a profane history of a profane people, a text whose holiness lies not in every word or page, or in every event or statement it recorded, but in the general movement of history it expressed, the movement which culminated in the advent of Jesus.

For the Jews, this posed a terrible dilemma. To hold their old view of scripture as revealed verbatim to and written by Moses is to go counter to science, history, and reason. To accept the findings of science and history is to sack the foundation of the Jewish faith. None of the luminaries of the period - Isaac Jost, Leppold Zunz, Solomon Steinheim, Samuel Holdheim- could find a way out. The inevitable conclusion pressed itself upon the minds of Jews: If the law of Judaism is the work of men - talented but human- of different times and places, it could not escape the relativity of history. Its validity, therefore, is rela- tive too, and hence, restricted. Indeed, there is little or no reason why its cumbersomeness may not be removed, and its provisions altered to fit the new situation. The whole normativeness of the law fell into question and the law was altered or violated with impunity.

With Abraham Geiger, the greatest of Reform thinkers, the last step was taken when he raised the question of the relation of Judaism to the ethnic entity of the Jews. His Hegelianism suggested to him that universalism and ethnocentrism were two contradictory theses whose dialectical opposition was necessary for human progress. Ethnocentrism, he reasoned, had fulfilled its purpose in the past. In modern times, it should have no place in the Jewish heart. Therefore, Geiger counselled, all references in the Bible to the election, distinctiveness, or particularism of the Jews, must be excised and repudiated. He reinterpreted Jewish messianism as referring not to a national saviour but to an age where all humans would cooperate together for their greater happiness and felicity.

To the question, what course should a Reform congregation pursue, Samuel Adler, noted American Reform Jew, answered: "The first and most important step is to free its service of shocking lies, to remove from its things and wishes which we would not utter if it had to be done in an intelligible manner. Such are the lamentations about oppression and persecution, the prayer for the restoration of the sacrificial cult, for the return of Israel to Palestine, the hope for a personal messiah, and for the resurrection of the body..." (David Philipson, The Reform Movement in Judaism, New York, Macmillan, 1907, p. 483). All the above-mentioned recommendations of Reform leaders the Pittsburgh Conference of 1885 enacted as a constitution for Reform Judaism; notably, legitimising the Jew's rejection of verbatim revelation of the Bible, of all Jewish laws not adapted to modern civilisation, dietary laws, laws concerning priestly purity, and of Jewish exclusivism on the religious, cultural and social levels.

It is not surprising that Reform thinking reached its most daring level in America, where there was no "ghetto" tradition. It was hence unavoidable that American Jews would assimilate the most, that assimilation would continue to corrode Jewish identity until hardly anything of it is left. As one American rabbi observant of the scene put it: "America is a terrible drain on Jewish identity; but the American university is for it a disaster area." The fact is that under the corrosive influence of secularism and assimilation, Judaism became in America little more than the arbitrary decision of the Jew to be different, not in fact to be different, but only to think of himself as different.

Reaction to the Reform line of thinking was strong but had little to offer besides conservatism, or the will to preserve the tradition. Intellectually this is not a happy alternative; for the contradiction essential to the nature of Judaism and that of modernity is not solved, but an attempt is made to live with it in complacency. Modernity, with its scientific objectivity and relativization of all history, has brought an irreversible orientation to the mind of the Jew. For him to hold to the letter of scripture as well as to the gains of modernity constitutes an insoluble dilemma. Max Lilienthal, David Einhorn and Bernard Felsenthal have all put it most aptly, in a language reminiscent of Theodore Parker, the father of Unitarianism. Law, they held, has a spirit and a body. The former is the decalogue, or the moral law innate to man's consciousness. The rest is the body. The Talmud is that body. It can be only buried once the spirit has left it. Furthermore, if we ought to deny the divine laws themselves once they have lost their spirit and effectiveness, we ought to deny, a fortiori, the Talmudic laws which we know to have been the dated and hence dead - works of human rabbis of bygone ages.

Had this trend continued to develop in Europe and America without interruption, Judaism might well have become a religious movement little distinguishable from the numerous other forms of pietism engendered by the "Radical Reformers" of Christianity. As it might be expected, there would have always remained some conservatives who could live with the contradiction. But with the overwhelming majority of Jews in West Europe and America subscribing to Reform thinking, the major currents of Jewish life and thought would have followed the same course. The Russian Revolution of 1918 would have given this movement tremendous impetus because the goals of

Reform Judaism would have accorded beautifully with the total assimilation objective of Russia, as well as with its goal of secular revolutionary progress.

History, however, had other goals.

Chapter IV:
The Romantic Relapse of Europe

A. Russian Pogroms

The prognosis of the last paragraph (Chapter III) was the reality on the American scene. Most of the rabbis ministering to the Jews of America were educated in the Reform seminaries of Europe, and the first seminary in America (Cincinnati, Ohio) belonged to the same group. The absence of persecution and of ghettos and the religious freedom guaranteed by the American Constitution promoted acculturation and assimilation of Jewish immigrants from Europe. In America, it was hard to be anything but a Reformed Jew. The voice of orthodoxy, of traditionalism, was certainly present; but it was overwhelmed by the universalism and secularism of American society in the matter of religion. The situation radically changed in the nineties when a wave of pogroms in Russia and Eastern Europe sent a flood of Jewish immigrants to America. The demography of American Jewry was turned upside down. In a decade, American Jewry became overwhelmingly ortho- dox and the voice of Reform Judaism became that of a minority. What happened in Russia to bring about this Jewish exodus happened in various degrees in the rest of Europe.

The Enlightenment never took root in Russia. Enlightenment ideas relevant to science, to trade, and industry, did. These ideas, mixed with deep mystical hopes for national restoration and produced the Europeanising industrialisation of Peter the Great. The outcome of this nineteenth century process was a surge of "Mother Russia" feeling coupled with a secularising will to progress. As to the Jews who up till then were living as strange aliens in city and village, the surge could only lead to their Russification. The movement produced some strong advocates' Peretz Smolenskin, Leo Pinsker, etc. - to persuade the Jews to russify themselves-a transformation as difficult to achieve for the Russian Jews, as it was for Russian Christians to promote perseverently.

The main reason why the Enlightenment proved to be a very indigestible novelty was the unpreparedness of the Russian mind. Russian experience was radically different from that of Western Europe. At last, as far as the intelligentsia is concerned, if not the majority of the people, the Russian Church was as guilty as the Catholic Church in the exercise of her dominion. That is why the forces of progress could countenance neither courtship nor alliance with the Church. Moreover, the Church -saw-and did so rightly-that the new movement for progress threatened her own power and therefore did everything it could to oppose and retard it. That is why the new movement leaned farther away from the Church, toward secularism. Furthermore, Christian Russia had no tradition of religious reform, no tradition of Renaissance, scholastic, Cartesian or Enlightenment rationalism. Whatever Enlightenment ideas the Russians of the nineteenth century had were borrowed from Western Europe. And since the whole of Napoleonic Europe was pitted against Russia, the borrowed ideas had to be adopted if and only after they have been fused into the overall "Russia" feeling. As for the Jews, the overwhelming majority of them were, like their Christian neighbours, still living in the crass ignorance of the Dark Ages. It was as if modernity had suddenly burst upon them. It is not surprising therefore that they neither understood nor accepted the Christians' half- hearted emancipation of them. The event of modernism was dazzling to both Christian and Jew.

This context explains why the Russian Christian's demand for Russification was not an "invitation," not an "emancipation," but rather an ultimatum. When heeded, it brought quick results, as when Jews quickly rose to highest rank in the service of Czar and country. But when it was received with hesitancy, no time was lost in patient acculturation. The Enlightenment's ideas of tolerance and reasonableness were quickly transformed into resentment and hate. In little time, even as the Jews were russifying themselves, the most violent pogroms broke out against them without apparent reason or cause. This sad Russian outcome was equally that of Jewish emancipation in Western Europe, but not for the same reason.

B. European Persecution

1. *The Ideational Groundwork*

Ever since it triumphed over paganism, the Christian Church had stood for the ideal of the universal community. It expanded itself as religion as well as worldly dominion under the aegis of that ideal; and, in fact, it was well suited toward that objective ever since Jesus had decreed: "God is indeed capable out of these stones to raise children unto Abraham" and Paul, "By one Spirit are we all baptised into one body, whether we be Jews or Gentiles, whether we be bond or free" (Matthew 3:19; 1 Corinthians 12:13). The Reformation gave the coup de grace to Christianity's ideal of the universal community. In fact, the Reformation was the result of a storm which, gathering long before, was only triggered by Luther's proclamation of the 95 theses. The numerous peoples of Europe rallied around their princes in order to shake off the authority of the Catholic Church, an authority which had become a "Byzantine" yoke, full of corruption, full of evil, bearing little or no resemblance to the universalist ideal it claimed itself to be.

Instead of this worthy Christian ideal, the emerging Protestant leadership tilted toward congregationalism to justify its breaking away from the Mother Church. But congregationalism itself needed justification, and this was sought in some- thing outside the Church when ecclesiastical history could not be found to support it. The Renaissance had already impressed the leadership with naturalism and the road lay open for a justification of the new religious autonomy with values intrinsic to the congregation as a distinct and separate human unit. These feelings constitute the germs out of which nationalism grew in Europe. In its prince and dynasty, each new autonomous Protestant congregation began to see a focus around which the people could rally to form the "nation" as a super-entity destined to carry out a "holy" mission of self-realisation. This contributed heavily to the growth of the centralised monarchies, and, in turn, gave the social cohesion necessary to keep the burgeoning European city together and its population attached to the "national" government. European nationalism grew as the universalism of the Church receded; and, by the end of the eighteenth century, it was strong and mature enough to give the Enlightenment and its political offspring - the world-order of the French Revolution - the most violent counter-action.

The Enlightenment preached its rationalism to Europeans already committed to Christian dogma as well as to Renaissance naturalism. These were too ingrained in Europe's consciousness for pure rationalism to succeed. Hence, practically all Enlightenment thinkers compromised rationalism to make room for both the Christian faith and naturalism. If this compromise could not be effected on the level of pure reason, then it was done on that of practical reason and judgment. Immanuel Kant, the prince of the Enlightenment, lectured on geography and international relations, where universal rationalism did not stop him from predicating a "natural" inferiority to the Asian races, nor from asserting that to be black is an argument. Instead of purging it of such compromise or aberration and hence making the Enlightenment more viable and stronger, the next generation of Europeans suspected and repudiated it altogether. Theirs was a failure of nerve; for they could not countenance what lay at the end of the road the Enlightenment opened, namely rationalist repudiation of Christian dogma along with the Church's authority which the Reformation had attacked, and universalist repudiation of ethnocentrism in favour of a world order founded on the equality of all mankind. Against the Enlightenment therefore, they levelled argument after argument which sought to redefine man in terms of ethnic history, language, and race. Blood or life, the earth with its plains, mountains, rivers and forests, and a vague past in the myths and legends of the Middle Ages, became the elements out of which the new ideology was constituted.

Evidently, such elements are not properly conceived by reason. They are the object of feeling and human instinct. A worldview built upon reason has no room for them; but one built upon them cannot only satisfy the trend toward naturalism (what could be more empirical than nature?) but allow plenty of room for accommodation of Christian dogma on the experiential basis of immediate feeling. The genius of Friedrich Schleiermacher was one of exchanging a crumbling foundation of the faith-universal reason for the solid one of personal experience, of ineffable feeling. The "Romantic" revolution was in full swing. The arts - literature, painting, sculpture, and music - were already filling the European mind with visions of a new order in which each ethnic group saw itself as the vortex of human history, a manifestation of the absolute on earth. Pregnant with the hopes engendered by a century of rationalism and universalist humanism, the con- science of Europe welcomed the Revolutionary army of Europe as a genuine "emancipating" force. But it turned cynical when that force disclosed the ugly head of France's imperialism, and surrendered itself with spite to its romantic enemy. The national wars which engulfed Europe in the sequel were the insane attempts of a sick man trying to cure himself of his disease with more of the same.

How could the Jew fit into this new order? Under a universalism based on reason rather than religious affiliation, the Jew was given a place where he could contribute to the public welfare, the commonwealth, or universal utility. But under a nationalism based on the romantic feeling of unity, of sharing in a mystical experience of common history, of communion with a particular "mother earth," of participation in a Christian tradition of values, he was most definitely an alien. The European Jew himself oft led and contributed to this romanticism, for its affinity with an age-old ethnocentrism of his own, the "Chosen People" complex. But his service only accelerated his own doom. For in the eye of the European Christian, the forces of a new rejection of the Jew as a foreign body were gathering momentum. It was only a matter of time before these would explode into political action. The transformation brought about by romanticism presented the European to himself as rooted in a given blood and soil and grown under a legacy of Christian values. Whether believer, secularist or atheist, he acknowledged the legacy to be constitutive, regardless whether he saw it as God-given or man-made. This marked the birth of a secularising Western culture which stood proud of its Christian heritage and indeed identified with it though on grounds other than those of traditional religious faith. Whether Catholic, Protestant, or atheist, Europeans agreed that Jewish identity was unassimilable with their own.

2. *Socio-Political Repulsion*

This intellectual repulsion of Jewish identity was prior to the socio-political. The latter was fired by the Jews' extraordinary success in taking advantage of Europe's tolerance and freedom. Jewish communal solidarity was forged under the white-hot fire of persecution throughout the millennia. It could not disappear in a spring or summer of emancipation. The Jews therefore obtained the goods, paid a fair portion of the price, but not the full settlement. As the Industrial Revolution swept over Europe, they assumed prominent roles in its leadership in all fields, production, finance, trade, communications, professions, research and the university. This was to provide the anti- Jewish demagogues of Europe with grist for their mills, and to project an image of the Jew as the villain of the system, the culprit in the mass movement for social justice, the future scapegoat of their anger and rebellion following national wars and crises.

Jew-hatred spread everywhere throughout Europe. Threatened by the Jews' rapid ascendancy in all fields of human endeavour, the Christian bourgeoisie of Europe unleashed one wave after another of anti-Jewish agitation. The factory, the marketplace, the army, the university, the government - every area of public life experienced repeated occurrences of anti-Jewish outbreaks. No country in Europe was safe. Most notorious was the Dreyfus affair in France, and most violent were the pogroms of the Poles and Russians against their Jews who were not yet out of their urban ghettos. Necessity was already at work in full force to reverse the

Enlightenment and the Emancipation it brought about in its trail. Ethnocentrism was more narrow-minded than the old rejection based on religion, and more violent. At its apogee in national socialism, it did not envisage its task as one of restricting the Jews to their numerical substance, nor to return them to their ghettos devoid of civic liberties, but of bringing about a "final solution" to their problematic existence in Europe.

Chapter V:
ZIONISM: The European Jew's Counsel of Despair

A. Between the Two Horns of a Terrible Dilemma

The Jews of Europe found themselves in the second half of the nineteenth century tossed on the horns of a terrible dilemma. If they pursued the gains of emancipation, they must assimilate; and the more they did so, the more their Judaism would have to be reformed, the more dilute it would become, the less Jewish they would finally turn out to be. If, on the other hand, they restricted their pursuit of the gains of emancipation and hence, the less they assimilated and lost thereby their Jewishness, the more they would stand out as strangers in a society bent on not granting them its identity. On either count, they stood to lose. But which loss was greater? Jewishness, or freedom, and often, life? It was not the conservative orthodox Jew of Russia that asked this ominous question, for he had never known freedom and the centuries had taught him that it is his fate to remain true to every letter of the Torah and to suffer - even die because of it. Rather, it was the Reform Jew of Western Europe who had tasted the joys and acquired the gains of freedom, who enthusiastically accepted the invitation to become English, French, or German but, at the same time, had to suffer new waves of persecution and hatred for doing so. Was it possible that Christian Europe had gone mad? The hyphenated Jew (English-Jew, French-Jew, German-Jew, etc.) could not understand what was happening to and around him.

Such a hyphenated Austrian-Jew was Theodor Herzl (1860-1904), a correspondent of the Vienna based Neue Frei Presse newspaper. Herzl belonged to Reform Judaism and was completely

Westernized. The dilemma of Jewish existence did not haunt his mind, convinced as he was that his personal destiny as well as that of his people was 'Europe.' Certainly, he knew of many lapses by Jews of their Judaism, and by Christians of their tolerance. But these did not bother him. Assigned to cover the trial of Dreyfus in Paris, he travelled thence with the intention of discovering new ways for Jewish-Christian cooperation and understanding. The facts glaring out of the case, however, taught him otherwise. The Dreyfus case established beyond doubt that the Christians were not at all committed to accepting the Jews in their midst no matter how Europeanised they may become. Who could suspect Dreyfus's Frenchness? his loyalty to the Republic? And yet, the very guardians of the Re- public were precisely the first to reject him. Adding insult to injury, Maurice Barrès, leader and spokesman for this anti- Jewish sentiment, had boldly defined patriotism as love of the past, France as a "collective being" which lives and speaks in the conscience of its sons, and national identity as communion of personal will with this Hegelian God-state and as harmony with it.

B. Zionism: Attempted Escape from the Dilemma

The Dreyfus episode, the upheaval it caused in France and Europe, and the awesome popularity of the anti-Jewish sentiment, left Herzl utterly dazed and dismayed, his hopes shattered and his ideal in ruins. It convinced him that the "European-Jew" ideal is impossible and futile. Since he himself was a European, educated under the same Hegelian romanticism dominating the university and cultural life of Europe, he really believed that the tendencies reflected at the Dreyfus trial were real and necessary forces of history which could not be stopped. No amount of assimilation was going to win for the Jew a European identity as long as he remained something to be assimilated, i.e., a Jew. In that direction, only conversion to Christianity would do, provided the milieu still believed in Christianity. Where that milieu had become scientific, skeptical and atheist, where it had replaced God with the state or "la nation," the ultimate base was blood and soil from which the Jew was excluded ex hypothesis. On the other hand, no amount of self-preservation could guarantee the Jew's survival in the midst of lands infested with this enemy mentality.

The solution of this dilemma readily presented itself to Herzl, the European romantic. There could be no return to the ghetto of the past. Therefore, the Jew must pick up his roots from Europe and leave. He must find for himself a place on this globe where he could be both a Jew and a free man; where he could exercise his Jewish identity in security; where he could allow his peculiar ethnic genius to blossom and maintain his dignity. For Herzl, it did not matter where this Jewish state was to be. In fact, he thought the Jewish state could be founded in Argentina; and he seriously considered Uganda, as well as Russian Central Asia, as possible sites. Palestine did receive a mention, but on a par with all those other possible areas of the world. Any place on earth or on the moon would do, provided it assured security and freedom for the Jew to be a Jew. The Jewish state which Herzl envisioned was not based on religion. It was to be a copy of the European secular national state, the only state he knew. Such a state would carry its own mystique, like the European original; it would enthrone a Jewish collective and pursue a Jewish community-destiny (Schicksalsge - meinschaft). A religious state, or a messianic restoration à la Isaiah of the Kingdom of David, was at the farthest possible remove from his mind. He expressly denied that the present predicament of the Jews in Europe was caused by Christianity.

Though true of the past, this was not true of the present attitude which Herzl regarded as due in the main to the socio-economic success of the Jews in the modern industrialised city. It is the Europeans' persecution of the Jews, he held, that makes the Jews a people; their persistent hatred of the Jews that creates the cohesiveness of the Jewish people. Herzl's Jewish state was an ideal born out of the gentiles' hatred and persecution of the Jews and the Jews' acculturation by the gentiles' romantic, nationalist, secularist God-state idea which dominated Europe at the time. His famous statement, "The [Jewish] state is already founded, in essence, in the will of the people of the state" is a perfect embodiment of that gentile, non-Semitic, indeed pagan god-state idea. This was equally the way Max Nordau, Herzl's successor, thought ("Zionism," in A. Hertzberg, ed., *The Zionist Idea*, New York, Atheneum, 1971).

It is difficult to say which of the two parent-conditions gave more than, or was prior to, the other in bearing Zionism as a solution to the tragedy of the European Jew. Certainly, persecution and hatred are negative. What they give birth to is of the nature of a reaction; and it is natural herd-feeling to withdraw into the group in face of danger. Necessarily, this is not creative; it is an "unvision." It is otherwise with the God- state, collective being idea of romanticism. It is a vision of reality, new and positive, which has the power to fascinate as well as to transform. It spread in Europe like wildfire; and the Jew, in his effort to Europeanise himself, fell into it with gusto. Herzl's mind which first articulated the vision of a Jewish state was thoroughly trained in it. But the first to envisage it were those Jews who lived in areas of Europe where the craving for a national entity was at its fiercest - namely, the Balkans and Poland. Yehudah Alkalai witnessed the movements of the Balkan peoples for national independence and sovereignty and envied them for their success. Zvi Kalisher participated in the struggle of the Poles and convinced himself that the Jews ought to do likewise to achieve an identical goal. The revolutionary movements of the mid-century which called for social justice in the name of national collectivism, inspired Moses Hess, another leading Zionist thinker, to mix up the Jew's yearning for egalitarian justice with a fatherland on the European model. Running against the grain of all Semitic wisdom through the ages in its assertion that "the People" has always meant solely the humans composing it, Moses Hess declared that "A common native soil is a precondition for healthier relations between capital and labour among the Jews" ("Comments," in The Zionist Idea, p. 136).

The same despair which characterised Herzl and the Jews of Western Europe filled the hearts of Eastern European Jews after the pogroms of 1871 and 1881. Peretz Smolenskin, while advocating with one side of his mouth that "every Jew is a citizen of the land in which he dwells, and it is his duty to be a good citizen [a citizen upon whom fall] all the obligations of citizenship like all other nationals," advocated with the other side of his mouth the theory that the Jews already had a "national identity" whose essence was culture. He claimed that the Jews "have always been a spiritual nation, one whose Torah was the foundation of its statehood." After 1881. Smolenskin dropped the European citizenship idea to advise his fellow countrymen to pull out their roots and emigrate to Palestine, for "only in the Land of Israel... can the Jews find truth and lasting peace" ("Let Us Search Our Ways." in The Zionist Idea, p. 151).

Likewise, Leo Pinsker advocated more than any Russian the total russification of the Jews of Russia and founded societies to bring about such assimilation. His dedication to the task and devotion to Mother Russia were noticed - and rewarded - by the Czar himself. Indeed, he was so blindly committed to Russification that even the pogroms of 1871 did not shake him. But the pogroms of a decade later did it. His assimilationist ideal was shattered, and he fell headlong into abandonment of Europe for the sake of a Zionist kingdom-to-be.

C. Europe's Failure of Nerve

The above-mentioned cases leave no room for doubt that the emancipation of the Jews was, as far as the Europeans are concerned, a half-hearted affair. It came "too little," and "too late" to establish itself securely in the legal and political systems of Europe whose people had been only "half-baked" by the Enlightenment. As to those Europeans who used their reason and were convinced of emancipation as a necessary corollary of their rationalism, their hearts were never won. For too long, the European stood unaffected by any sentiment of universal humanity or fraternalism. Equally, the emancipation of the Jews had come too late; for, the forces of ethnocentrism. nationalist self-assertion and egotism were too deeply impressed upon the European soul for the Enlightenment to undo. Though temporarily silenced by the military and political might of Revolutionary France and fastened securely by legislation, this European ethnocentrism reacted violently once these stops were removed by the retreat of Napoleon.

Furthermore, there is no room for doubt that the Emancipation of the Jews came too little and too late as far as the Jews were concerned. It came too little because the Europeans could not sustain it for more than a generation; and where they did sustain it at all, they did so reluctantly. The Jewish claim is certainly sound that whatever gains the Jews acquired were achieved by superior Jewish effort, never gratuitously given; that Jewish superiority in the various fields of endeavour was only the obverted façade of the Jews' ever-denied equality. On the other hand, the Emancipation came too late because the ghetto had reshaped the Jewish soul beyond the possibility of universalist reform; even beyond that of relaxing ethnocentrism to enable the Jews to coexist with their European hosts. The ghetto had built separatism into their flesh, as the diaspora had built it into their bones; and Biblical ethnocentrism had built it into their marrow. It was inconceivable therefore that the Emancipation would efface Jewish collectivism, or that this would happen within a generation.

The European thought he had fooled the Jews. When he began to discover that he was fooled by them, he lost his temper! He thought he could wipe the Jews off the map of Europe by Europeanising them; but he did so only for a moment, and he seems never to have been truly convinced of it. The Jew, too, thought he could wipe off European hatred by merely changing his name and language; but he did everything he could, working thrice as hard as anyone, to achieve quick mastery over his fellow Europeans, both as affirmation of his racial superiority and protection against insecurity. Each of them knew in his depth that the other was only fooling. The European's loss first of his "Enlightenment" nerve and, subsequently, of his "reason" in the romantic outbreak, convinced the Jews that their fears, which never left them - were certainly justified. Hence, the disillusionment and despair on both sides.

If, under the circumstances, the Jew opted for the Zionist solution of pulling out his roots and exiting from Europe, his decision is certainly understandable, though we may criticise it as one of despair. The plain truth was that the European soul was sick.

The cure did not lie in a Jewish exodus. Europe had nursed and sustained the ideal of the universal community for a millennium of Church ascendancy. This left an indelible, though temporarily submerged, mark upon its soul. What it needed was a restrengthening of the Enlightenment nerve that failed it. That is what the emancipated Jews of Europe should have helped restore and promote until it could blossom forth again. What they did, however, was the reverse. From their new positions of leadership in European life, they helped fan the very fires of romanticism which were later to consume them and ruin Europe.

No one will doubt that romanticism made the souls of Germany, France, Belgium, Holland, Italy, Poland, and the Balkan countries sing and dance with delight - nay, intoxication! No one will doubt that the arts of Europe blossomed as if in a hothouse; or that romanticism did something to promote science and technology under the heat of national defense; or to institute accord and harmony, social justice and welfare, between the members of the national group. Nor can it be denied that these were in some sense, human gains as well, indirectly relevant to the welfare of humankind.

But it cannot be denied that from the purview of human history, these songs and dances of romantic Europe were macabre; that the hothouse atmosphere engendered by romanticism detracted the soul of Europe farther away from God and His law. Romanticism dethroned God and apotheosised the state and the nation. It granted absolute priority to the common will because it is "common" and "actual." It agreed with John Stuart Mill that the only evidence that a thing is desirable is that it is desired and went on to mix up the success of nationalist egotism with divinity. It relativised all past history and destroyed its normativeness, while it absolutised the present which is no less dated than the past. With Schleiermacher, it dethroned "reason" and replaced it with "feeling." The religiously oriented were relieved that the new base of "feeling" and personal ineffable experience provided far sounder support for Christian dogma, then in peril from the attacks of rationalists as well as scientists and other secularist "despisers of religion." The secularly oriented, on the other hand, saw in "feeling" a new epistemological base for their romantic claims. They were thus emboldened to absolutise their particularist theses for "Volkstum," "national genius," race and Historismus, and they sought inspiration in a mystical experience of empirical nature. The innate contradictions of human tendencies and passions were enthralled as visions of the sublime. Romanticism asserted that the highest and ultimate expression of the human soul was tragedy - and Wagner! Fascism was romanticism's proudest offspring, secularism his throne. Hitler came down in the very flames it quickened, but not before Europe lay scorched and in ruins.

The greatest pity is that the victims of romanticism's holocaust of the last one hundred years, namely, the Jews, had become infected with the disease, and helped fan its flames by their literary, artistic, and philosophical contributions. But the pity that is greater than the greatest is that their walking skeletons should emerge from the Nazi ovens singing-as Zionists- an adapted romantic song of their own, whose materials may perhaps be Jewish but whose essence is Romanticism all over again, both *à la Treitschke and à la Wiesel*!

Chapter VI:
Jewish Universalism and Ethnocentrism

A. Distinguishing the Revelation from Its Text

From the standpoint of Islam, there can be no doubt that Abraham, Isaac, Jacob, Joseph, Moses, David, Solomon were all prophets whom God had sent forth with a divine message. There can be no doubt that that message was always one and the same in its essential content which consisted, above all, of the recognition of God, of His unity and transcendence, of the Day of Judgment, of the purposiveness of history, and of man's responsibility to manage space-time as God has directed. That the prescriptive laws God had revealed to these prophets differed somewhat from the earlier revelations made to previous prophets, is granted; but it is understood as belonging to the "how" of obedience and fulfilment rather than to the essence. Equally, there can be no doubt that the Torah is God's revelation to Moses, that it had definitively summed up and crystallized the earlier revelations. To doubt these facts is kufr, or unbelief.

To acknowledge the divine source of the Torah, however, is not to assert that the book currently known as the "Torah" is the exact and veritable text of the Torah revealed to Moses. For this, historical proof is needed; and critical history tells a completely different tale. It tells that the Torah was re-formed and re-written by scribes and priests under King Josiah in the seventh century B.C.; that it was recast by the Jewish priest- hood over many centuries; that it was lost or destroyed during the Exile in the sixth century; that it was rewritten by Ezra, the scribe, in the fifth, etc. Although some early Christians, notably Marcion and his followers in the third century A.C., doubted the religious value of the Torah as handed down to them and called upon Christians to reject it, the majority of Christians accepted it and incorporated it as part of an "Old Testament" which they juxtaposed with a "New Testament" written by the apostles of Jesus. Christian thinkers then overcame the un-Christian message of the Torah by interpreting it allegorically. Marcion and his warning were forgotten; and the claim for the integrity of the Torah would have gone unchallenged were it not for God's constant providence.

B. Two New Disciplines

It was Al Qur'an al Karim, the revelation sent to the Prophet Muhammad (SAAW), which first questioned the veracity, not of the Torah as such, but of the Torahic text. By its persistent questioning, by its indictment that the rabbis were even then and there, still "reforming" and "rewriting" the Torah to suit their needs and wishes, al Qur'ân has initiated a new discipline textual criticism - and a new science - the scientific study of religion. Practically every Muslim thinker thereafter participated in the new intellectual endeavour, then given the title of al Milal wa al Nihal ("Studies of Religions and Para-Religions"). In time, the discipline produced a number of giants, Ibn Hazm, al Baghdādī, al Nawbakhti. Of Ibn Hazm, orientalist Alfred Guillaume said that he anticipated Western Biblical critics by a whole millennium, even in the most minute of his criticisms of the Torahic text. Indeed, Western Biblical criticism began with Wellhausen, Kühnen and Graf, who were all Islamicists well acquainted with al Qur'an's critique of the Biblical text.

C. Universalist and Ethnocentrist Strands in Judaism

Any objective historian's examination of the Torah reveals that it is a text composed of many strata deriving from periods separated by hundreds of years; that its compilation must have been the work of centuries, thus repudiating once and for all the Jewish claim that the text of the Torah is verbatim revelation, as well as the Rabbinic claim, that that text is integrally the one given by Moses as revelation. Any unbiased reading of the text would also reveal that two main traditions have intertwined themselves in it, intercalating their precepts within its lines. Almost every Torahic narrative or exhortation speaks, as it were, with two mouths. These traditions can best be described as "universalist" and "ethnocentrist." They have characterised almost every passage of the Torah as well as of the other books of the Old Testament. This observation casts doubt upon the theory that the whole Old Testament is verbatim revelation; but it does not disprove that a fair part of it is in fact revelation. Indeed, such a distinction saves the revealed part and places it beyond attack thus providing a first advantage. Secondly, the distinction accommodates the critical historian's view that the scripture is a body of writings which came to be regarded by the adherent-interpreters as reflecting the living religious reality of their age, and hence were edited, rearranged, and refined under the influence of that reality. Thirdly, the distinction is wide enough to sustain the religious faith that working with a traditional text that is unquestionably revealed, reinterpretation and edition by later prophets and scribes constitute revelation, no less than the earlier phenomenon. This last advantage accommodates the most conservative view, which cannot escape the evidence of change in widely separated revelations through time, nor demand - religiously speaking - the total absence of change. Finally, the distinction narrows down the difference between the Jewish and Islāmic views.

Whereas Judaism claims revelation status for the earlier as well as the later texts, Islām affirms the earlier and rejects only the later.

The universalist strand differs substantially from the ethnocentric in their conception of divinity, of revelation, of piety, of the covenant, of the people or nation, of the Day of Judgment, of morality, of the place of Jerusalem and Palestine in the religion.

1. Divinity

In the universalist strand, God is One and Transcendent. He is the Creator of heaven and earth, Lord and Master, Sustainer and Judge of the universe. He is omniscient and omnipotent, loving, and merciful to all His creatures. This is amply supported by dispersed texts running from Genesis to Malachi. It is not the case that in the ethnocentrist strand any of these predicates is denied. They are not. They are all asserted and acknowledged as true. But in addition to them, other contradictory predicates, or predicates incompatible with the universalist conception of the deity, are ascribed. It is maintained that God may be addressed as Elohim, a plural of "god";[1] that the Elohim, or many gods, have come to earth and copulated with the daughters of men (Genesis 6:2); that "the gods" belong to someone in such a way that Jacob could steal them away from Laban (Genesis 31:30) and Leah could cover them with her skirts and sit on them (Genesis 31:34-35). The ethnocentrist strand holds that God wrestled physically with a human and lost the battle (Genesis 32:24-30); that God is subject to passion and to pity (Genesis 9:21); that He acts unjustly and is biased in favour of a tiny segment of humanity,

[1] The term is widely distributed throughout the whole Old Testament, pointing to an edition of the work wherein the references to God were changed to fit this appellation of the deity.

the Jews. The contrast is vividly painted between the universalist God Who is absolutely One and Transcendent, and the ethnocentrist God who is in every respect a "ghost" kind of God, a god of tribal animism. That is why Biblical scholars have reserved the name Judaism and Jewish religion to the later, post-Exilic manifestation, and "Hebrew religion" to the religion of the patriarchs as expressed in the Old Testament. Ethical monotheism, they claimed, is true of the later phenomenon, whereas monolatry is true of the earlier.

2. Revelation

The universalist strand maintains that God reveals His will to humankind that they may obey it; that revelation is the law of God equally incumbent upon all; that since the unity of God and the unity of truth are corollaries, revelation must be one and the same at least in essence; that differences in revelation from period to period or place to place always pertain to application rather than spirit of the law. Being from God, revelation is holy. Respect belongs to its spirit and letter, both of which are always public. This means that it is of the nature of revelation to proclaim and universalise itself. Its truths are never esoteric, and they can never be reached by mere eisegesis. Hence the text of revelation must be preserved along with the categories with which its meanings could be comprehended.

The ethnocentrist strand, *per contra*, conditions the revelation of God by the advantage it provides to the ethnic entity. Taking such relation as the raison d'être of revelation, it understands its normativeness not as universal, but as pertaining to the recipient ethnic entity alone, and hence, assumes the laws of God to apply only to the members, not to outsiders. The latter, ethnocentrism holds, may have their own revelation as it is possible for them to have their own god or gods. God is the "God of Israel," "of Abraham," "Isaac," "Jacob" and of their descendants. If He reaches out to the others, He does so not for their own sake but in order to vindicate, defend or avenge "His own people." Only they are "His sons," object of His loving care and mercy. The others can enjoy His care and mercy by derivation from, or association with, "His people." Obviously, for ethnocentrists, there can be in principle more than one revelation, that such revelations can be as radically varied as their recipients; for there are as many gods as there are ethnic entities. Even for an Isaiah, such other gods are weak, impotent, even nothing; but they are not not-gods. Certainly, they are lesser gods, but still gods, de jure (Isaiah 40:18ff; 41:22ff).

The necessary relation to ethnic entity justifies eisegesis of revelation to the end of realising the advantage of that entity. In another dimension, the same relation has granted revelation status to those historical writings (Chronicles, Kings) whose sole message is the affirmation and promotion of the ethnic entity. Indeed, the relation to the ethnic entity is reciprocal: What the entity does collectively, what happens to it, the unfolding of its destiny - that is equally revelation! The ethno- centrist view does not find contradition between its stand on revelation and universalism. It asserts both and seeks to realise whatever advantage lies in each of them.

The same necessary relationship to the ethnic identity affects the meaning of piety. Whereas the universalist view devotes all piety, all worship, and all majesty to God alone, and so orders human life as to make it possessed by the divine presence at every one of its moments, the ethnocentrist view raises the ethnic entity to the point of sharing the majesty of God, and the piety and worship of man. Thus, the religion itself is defined in terms of God, Law or Torah, and people. Devotion to "the people" becomes a corollary of devotion to God. The "Klal Israel" acquires a mystical halo because it becomes, in ethno- centrism, something numinous.

3. Covenant

Nothing illustrates this para-divine nature of the ethnic entity better than the understanding of the covenant in the two views. Under universalism, the covenant expresses the moral purpose of creation, the essence of human morality. It asserts that man, being created to the end of obeying God and fulfilling His will in creation, is free and capable to do so; that whether he does or does not obey is the criterion of his moral merit. Obedience to the divine imperative will issue in success in this world and blessedness in the next; disobedience, in failure and dam- nation. God's covenant, being moral, is universal and applies to all human beings. It is the "arrangement" or "pattern" by which God is pleased or displeased, the former when humans obey His laws, the latter when they are oblivious to them. The covenant of universalism is always a "two-way street": Man's moral obligation to God and the pattern of God's disposal of men's affairs. Under ethnocentrism, the covenant has lost its universal nature and consequently its moral character. It has become "the Promise" by which God has bound Himself to favour His People, and to continue to favour them regardless of their moral performance (Deuteronomy 7:6-8; Hosea 4:12). He chooses them and proffers His blessings upon them, vindicates, and avenges them, defends and gives them victory, not for their morality, but simply because He has bound Himself to them, and so because they alone are His People. That they are "hard and stiff necked," that they have gone a-whoring after other gods, does not matter because, according to the "Prophet" Hosea, they are still the "sons" of God and God is their "Father" (Hosea 11:8-9). Where ethnocentrism is unable to explain the tragic facts of history, when God's People have indeed suffered catastrophes, it acknowledges the event as a chastisement, a punishment inflicted for sins committed. But it can never countenance such option on the part of God as "And if the people turn away from this call, God will exchange them for another people who will not..." (Qur'an 47:38; 9:49). To this end, ethnocentrism has invented the doctrine of "the Remnant" (Isaiah 37:32), basing God's continued election and favouritism to the Jewish people on the claim that a small remnant of Jews have kept their loyalty and morality and thus justified the necessary favouritism (Zechariah 8:12). In fact, the theory also holds that the remnant cannot go wrong, that its virtue is always necessary (II Kings 21:14: Zephaniah 3:13). Its purpose is hence to provide another leg on which the doctrine of election stands; in case of difficulty, to play the role of a *deus ex machina.*

Confirming the inevitability of God's blessing to the Jews, ethnocentrism has interpreted the covenant in material, bio- logical and hence racist terms, and spoken of it as being "in the Flesh." Its symbol is circumcision (Genesis 17:9-14). This is only a symbol. It's being in the flesh is understood as something innate and hereditary, utterly independent of morality. The whole moral struggle is irrelevant to it. A Jew is a Berith (son of the covenant) even if he apostasies. As such, he remains entitled to God's favour, to elect status. It is on this basis that the State of Israel regards every Jew in the world as its citizen, regardless of whether he has decided to join or not. Even Alfred Rosenberg had to admit, when cornered, that "race" was ultimately a question of culture and values, and only preparatorily a question of cephalic index, blondness, etc. And the modern South African apartheid advocates define "white," "black" and "coloured" in such a way as to include the Japanese in the white class, the Syrians and Egyptians in the "black," and the Malaysians and Indonesians in the "coloured." Obviously, their need is to find a base other than the physical on which to find their discrimination. Not so with Jewish election and covenant. Moreover, the obvious racial diversity of male parents during two millennia of ghetto existence and persecution has caused the Government of Israel to define Jewishness in terms of biological maternal descendance.

4. The Jewish People, Morality, and the Day of Judgment

The universalist strand regards the Jewish People on a par with other creatures of God. If their history has been different, it is because God has chosen to send His messengers to teach and to warn them. Hence, they stand under greater obligation to be righteous. For those who know, who have been adequately taught and warned have far less excuse to do wrong, or even to err. They are, besides, God's ambassadors to mankind, or to their neighbours or next of kin. They must therefore exemplify the morality they profess. Their ambassadorship would thus be actualised. The Day of Judgment, for them, is the Day on which God would reckon with every human his past deeds, and judge mankind on a standard of absolute justice. Judgment is the keystone of morality, the logical consequence of freedom and responsibility.

On the other hand, ethnocentrism's view of the people, nation, or ethnicity is the key which determines its view of everything else. The ethnic entity is elevated to the highest level, but it is not fused with the deity, nor does it take its place. It becomes a prime associate of the deity, defining and channeling God's relation to the People. In consequence, the ethnic entity becomes the principal category on which morality, culture, law and civilization depend, and God becomes a constitutional figurehead. The entity's priesthood assumes the role of lawmaking, of governing, and of determining the life of the entity on earth. Being ethnic, the entity is necessarily earth- bound, and regards itself as eternal in time. It is not impressed by the Day of Judgment or the hereafter. It interprets the Day of Judgment as the Day on which it will be vindicated, revenged, against its earthly enemies, rather than the Day on which God reckons with all men their moral and immoral works and passes a judgment of reward or punishment to each on the basis of his or her own works.

5. Jerusalem, Palestine

Finally, the universalist strand regards Jerusalem and Palestine as accidental to revelation. It acknowledges the previous revelations of God to the prophets inhabiting that spot of earth and keeps a memory of joy and gratitude to God for having made the inhabitants of that spot of earth the recipients, or first audience, of revelation. It knows that God might have placed His revelation anywhere else; and that, had He done so, His revelation would be as normative and binding and excel- lent as before (Qur'an 6:124). Hence, it sees no causal relation whatsoever between the "real estate" and revelation, between the rocks of the ground and the deity. The same is true of the Kingdom of David of history. That kingdom has no value other than that which history assigns to it. Some aspects of it may well be worth emulating, especially those in which it has proved its obedience to God and His commandments. But it is never confused with Paradise, the other kingdom which is a spiritual, timeless and spaceless, a transcendent dependency of the transcendent God.

In ethnocentrism, *per contra,* Jerusalem and Palestine are pieces of real estate whose religious value is intrinsic to the physical aspect of their being, in addition to the spiritual memorial being recognized by universalism. Halévy, who is often quoted by the Zionists as a medieval predecessor, saw a causal relationship between the physical earth, air and water of Palestine and the divine dispensation. Actually, it should not come as a surprise that God Who has chosen a people in the flesh to be His favourite through their biological generation, that He chose a piece of real estate to be His "dwelling place" forever. Ethnocentrism was bold enough to tie the divine presence to Jerusalem. In the mouth of one of its prophets, viz., Nathan, it laid down the law that God could not be reached except in Jerusalem, that the Jew cannot worship Him unless he stands on Jerusalem's soil (II Samuel 7:4ff; I Kings 5:17; 8:27ff). Hence, all the attachment to the Eretz or soil which made any amount of it desirable as a guarantee of the connection to the Deity. Having ethnicised God by associating Him with the ethnic entity, eth- no-centrism enlandised Him and restricted Him to the physical historical frontiers of Jerusalem. For it, Jerusalem is not merely an expression of values to be remembered and observed, but a continuing physical reality to be possessed. Likewise, the Davidic Kingdom is a physical, political, social, military and economic kingdom reestablished on its own land. To the universalist formula that Judaism consists of God and His law or revelation, ethnocentrism adds "and His People" or the chosen ethnic entity, and "and the physical land." Even a Martin Buber, perhaps the most spiritualised of modern Zionists, could not resist the ethnocentric appeal. He declared that between land and people, and hence land and God, there is a mysterious connection of timeless proportion. Apparently, God, in ethnocentrism is not only the god of a tribe, a god in whose nature a particular tribe is inextricably embedded. He is equally the god of a land from which He is inseparable, and which is equally embedded within His nature in a mysterious way which passes understanding. Such is the logic of Jewish ethnocentrism.

D. Alternating Dominance of the Two Strands

Although the universalist and ethnocentrist strands have been present in Jewish consciousness, their history has known periods in which one or the other was dominant. Certainly, the Exilic Age (609-500 B.C.), the age of Hellenistic ascendency (200 B.C.-650 A. C.), the Islamic Period (650-1948), the West European Period of the Enlightenment (1650-1850), and the American Period (1650-1939), the Russian Communist period since 1918, are periods in which the universalising view dominated the thinking of the overwhelming majority of Jews in the territory in question. These periods had their own leaders who stand out prominently as advocates of universalism; namely, Jeremiah and Isaiah; Philo; practically all Jewish thinkers and leaders in the realm of Islam but notably Ibn Maymün, Sa'adiah and Hayyüy ibn Zakariyyā; Spinoza, Lessing, Mendelssohn, Geiger; Isaac Wise, David Kaufman, Einhorn and Kohler, etc., in respective order. Equally certain, the period of David's monarchy (990-922 B.C.), of Ezra and Nehemiah (549-440 B.C.), of the Maccabees (330 B.C.-70 A.C.), of Europe's Pre-Enlightenment ghetto-age (300-1650 A.C.), and of modern Zionism (1933 to the present are the periods in which ethnocentrism was the dominant view. Coming on the heels of the Enlightenment and in an age in which the Western world seems to have replaced God with the ethnic entity, the present rise of Jewish ethnocentrism is the strongest of all previous periods. Its phenomenon is worldwide and, so far at least, it has enjoyed the understanding and blessing of the

Western nations as a sister movement whose nature is very much like their own.

Chapter VII:
Zionism as Religion

A. The Romantic Base of all Zionists

Born out of Europe's Romantic lapse and anti-Jewish pogroms, Zionism might have occupied itself entirely with the question of Jewish security. At its genesis and for a long time afterwards, Zionism did little else besides seeking the real estate wherein to set up refuge from the dim future it foresaw. There is no evidence in early Zionist writing of any concern with the kind of problems faced by the Reform movement, and in search of a solution of which, the movement was born. The first leaders did not think in terms of the problems science and modernity posed to the application of the laws of the Shulhan Arukh, which dominated Jewish observance and living since its codification by Joseph Karo in 1567. The whole problem of "religion and modernity" did not occupy them at all. The Zionists were men and women nursed culturally and spiritually by a secular Europe which has been weaned away from religion. They were as immersed in romanticism and secularism as their fellow Christians; and a number of them were in fact leaders of the movement in Europe. It was therefore natural that, once renewed persecution blocked their self-identification as European, the Jews would seek their identity in their tradition, and that they would do so under the only categories they knew, namely, those of European romanticism.

A return by the West European Jew to the letter of the Bible was forever closed by the ravages to the text of revelation which Biblical criticism had brought about. Based on feeling and will, romanticism provided an easy escape. With ease and readiness, it combined itself with the tendency to secularise to which most educated Europeans were prone, and it provided a stance from which even the letter of scripture could be reinstated as religiously significant. This stance, the romantic interpretation of religion and history, was buttressed by a modernist epistemology of relativist cultural intuitionism. All history, romanticism held, was a reflective mirror in which the author and his ethnic entity read themselves, their wishes and hopes; and there is no historical reality to be sought or established outside this figuration. History, in short, is a moment of self-reflection in the stream-of-the-manifold of group consciousness. Its products, the books of history, are interpretations, as it were by definition, whose veracity depends not on their correspondence with the past itself, but on the adequacy of their rendering of the blik of the generation in which they are written. Every generation, indeed, every writer, may have his own blik from which to view the past, and every blik is legitimate. In accord with this theory, Zionism could afford to be literalist, accommodating the fundamentalist orthodoxy's position by adhering to the verbatim validity of scripture while rejecting the doctrine of verbatim revelation in favour of the vague and woozy theory of the "God Who Acts in History." Christian Protestant theologians had previously done so for the same reason. The Biblical scribe, the theory holds, was not a recorder of revealed text but the "redactor" of a vision experienced by his contemporaries and ineffably felt by them to be the truth of the moment of history in question. Hence, Zionists agree with the naive that every letter of scripture is true; but, unlike the naive, they hold its truth derivable from the reality of the feeling of those whose feeling it expressed.

This romanticism goes beyond the dispute between the religious Zionists, such as Yehiel Pines and Abraham Kook, and the secular Zionists, such as Herzl, Jacob Klatzkin, Ahad Ha'am, Weizmann, and Ben Gurion. Indeed, it is the common ground on which all of them stand. For all of them are, properly speaking, romantics. Their vision envelops the whole past and future of the Jewish people. It is refined by the lessons they learned from Romantic Europe. The function of history, the relativism of truth, the roles of feeling and will, the Weltans- chauung and its comprehensiveness; Volkstum and its place in culture, the *Lebensraum* and *Blut und Boden* mystique, the here- now populist salvation, the idealisation of nature - all these lessons the Zionists have learnt only too well, for the insights they provided were to be utilised as a filter screen through which Jewish history and religion are to be seen and apprehended.

The "religious Zionists" looked upon Zionism as a program of socio-political, economic, and military action designed for the purpose of actualising an essence which is the religious content of Judaism. Monotheism, the Law, justice, and peace, a world order based upon them, symbolically expressed by the restoration of the Jews within that world order, but at its centre, is their ultimate goal. The conservative orthodox Jews who rejected Zionism did so not because they did not share the goal, but because they regarded it as eschatological, as something to be brought about by God alone, at His desire as well as by His efficiency, not those of men. The religious Zionists agreed with this, but held what appeared blasphemous to the non-Zionists, viz., that the miracle of God needed man's work for it to happen. Religious Zionism is religious nationalism, the will to preserve and promote the ethnic entity for the sake of the content of Judaism. Nationalism here remains the means, spiritual content of the religion, the end. Romanticism cemented the two and made them interdependent. Its guilt in Islamic religious terms is exactly what the Qur'an has meant by "shirk," or associationism, i.e., the associating of other beings with God as Ruler of Creation and hence, Maker of History.

B. Secular Zionism

Secular Zionism defined the religion in terms of nationalism, claiming that the religion is merely an expression of the nationalist spirit. "Judaism is nationalism," it exclaimed, and it sought to reduce the religious dimension of Judaism to phenomena of a subjective group consciousness determined by its own vision of itself. As the living condition of a subjective consciousness, Jewish nationalism does not depend upon the sharing of the content of religion. It is perfectly possible even among committed atheists. It rests on the objective fact-consciousness predetermined by past Jewish history - and an act of willing to continue to be part of the Jewish People. Gemeinschaft and Gesellschaft are at the same time its twin bases, and both have nothing to do with religion except a loose, accidental, and severable association. Jewishness, according to the secular Zionists, depends upon "form," not "content;" not whether God is worshipped and what law is observed, but how religion is practiced. "Form" as a constitutive modality is of the essence of romanticism. Secular Zionism agrees fully because under this modality it can give priority and pre-eminence to the political will and relegate to unimportance the God and Torah of Israel in which it does not believe anyway, but to which it can nonetheless assign a useful function. Repudiating the classical content-definition of Jewishness as belief in God and observance of His Torah (law), secular Zionism redefined it in terms of "form." What makes a Jew Jewish, it maintained, is neither his belief in God nor observance of His law, but how he lives his Jewishness. The only "how" secular Zionism recognises as fulfilling its ideology is the "territorial-political definition of Jewish nationalism" by which it does not mean the possession of a base for national life, but the be-all and end-all of national- ism, for "living on the land is ipso facto the national life" (Jacob Klatzkin, "Boundaries" in The Zionist Idea, pp. 318-319).

Obviously, God and Torah are superfluous here and can be dispensed with, though they can do no harm if they exist. The masses, always naive and "religious" may even need them. Henceforth, they are to become symbols expressing the only *facta* romanticism holds dear: soil, blood, and the feeling of community and destiny. Obviously, too, God and His law are here dethroned, and the ethnic entity has replaced them. It is to the thought of Martin Buber that Zionism owes this theological transformation. In his view, revelation is not what God has given, but what an individual man has experienced and communicated to his fellows who have understood and appreciated. This makes revelation equivalent to lived group experience in which God, the prophet and the revealed content are all instruments of an ethnic entity's coming into self-consciousness. Indeed, for Buber, revelation is history and history is revelation. But he has the Hegelian temerity to call this "humanity touched by the divine." Indeed, he regarded the ethnic identity convertible with God Himself (subhānahu wa ta'ālā 'ammā yushrikun!). The "Song of Deborah" he regarded as the perfect mirror of this thought of his because it "expresses a fundamental reality by repeatedly alternating the name of this God with the name of Israel, like a refrain." To make things still worse, i.e., to dispel any spiritual understanding of the concept "Israel" so as to make it in any way include all the righteous members of humankind besides the Jews, Martin Buber, the most "spiritual" of the Zionists, claims that Israel is itself impossible without the rocks, sand and water that are Palestine. For, he asserts, the very "being" of Israel lies in "the holy matrimony of land and people." With still greater bravado, Buber goes on to claim for this connection of "real estate" with Israel "a unique category... touching the universally human, the cosmic and even of Being itself" (Israel and Palestine, p. x).

Buber's case is not one of simple shirk or association of other beings with God. It is a sin unknown to the pre-Islamic Arabs, a sin condemned so vehemently by the Old Testament itself, namely, the identification of God with nature, of the Creator with the creature, the predication of transcendence to nature. The Ancient Egyptians, the Philistines, Canaanites, Assyrians and Babylonians, and finally the Greeks and Romans, were condemned by Judaism, its prophets, or scripture for doing precisely this. Modern time is witness to the Zionist Jews perpetrating identically the same sin à la Georg Friedrich Hegel.

C. Zionism: A Strictly European Experience

Evidently, both the religious and the secular Zionists share the Romantic *Weltanschauung* and do not differ from each other except in degree. Both of them equally hold to the view that feeling, or subjective consciousness, is the ultimate determiner of reality, that the ultimate category in this determination of reality is the ethnic entity, whether dis-enlandised but in process or re-enlandisement, as in religious Zionism, or imperfect and inexistent until enlandised, as in the secular variety.

Evidently, Zionism, the consequence of European persecution and European romanticism, is an experience of European Jews alone. Only reluctantly, one might yet accept the claim that American and Russian Jews are heirs to European history and share in it, though the former have known no persecution. But one cannot accept this predication of Russian Jews. For, they have known neither real enlightenment nor extensive emancipation until the Communist Revolution. In another direction, no one in his senses would accept predication of such experience to non-Western Jews, whose history and experience have known neither persecution, nor mass pogroms, neither enlightenment nor romanticism, neither the French Revolution nor Hegel. Of these, the Jews of the Muslim World who have produced the Golden Age of Jewish thought and philosophy, of Hebrew literature and linguistics, and did so under the aegis of Islām, are especially remarkable. That Zionism had by agitation, luring appeal or subversion, attracted two million of these Oriental Jews, uprooted them from their traditional homes and brought them as refugees to Palestine, can in no way be ever condoned. For, the experience out of which Zionism was born, and to which it came as answer; the Romantic cultural phenomenon under the aegis of which it was conceived, and under which the Zionist reinterpretation of Jewish religion, culture and identity has taken place - all this is foreign to them. It is anything but justice to impose this "Europeanism" upon them. And it is a sinister crime to "re-educate" and "acculturate" or better, to "Westernise" - them into it. It contains all the important elements of a spiritual genocide. The wonder is all the greater that this is happening under the guise of "restoration", of "religious messianism." If Western Jews may be entitled to their own disease, a fortiori Oriental Jews must be entitled to their own sanity. The Islamic atmosphere in which they have lived for centuries which encouraged and helped nourish their notion of divine transcendence and of election as morality and righteousness, should continue to do so if Judaism is to remain a member of the Semitic family of religions.

Chapter VIII:
Zionism as Politics

A. Before World War I

At its early stage, Zionism considered central Asia, still newly annexed by Czarist Russia, which was anxious to colonise it, as a possible Zion in which the Jews would dwell, and Zionism would fulfil itself. When this turned unworkable and Zionist leadership became attached to the bandwagon of the British Empire, Uganda was considered. However, its black population and neighbourhood were too un-European for a racist's comfort. It too was dropped, and Zionist attention focussed on Palestine, an integral part of the Ottoman Empire. So, Herzl went to Istanbul to "buy" Palestine off from its "master," the Sultan. When he turned down the offer, Herzl resorted to threats against the Empire as a whole, which he knew his British and other western partners had been longing to defeat, dismember, and devour.

Herzl's threats did not work, and his political proposition was flatly turned down. He pleaded on the religious level, and begged that some Jews who are religiously committed to live and die in Palestine in proximity to the holy places which they cherish, be allowed to enter, to buy land and settle, and to live as integrated citizens of the wide world of Islam like so many of their Jewish brothers and sisters who are already living in most Muslim cities, and in Istanbul itself. Such a proposition could not be turned down because of the constitutional guarantee which the Islamic State granted to its non-Muslim citizens. What commended it most was the fact that it was not a political scheme but a humanitarian and religious one. Moreover, it was not the first time that Jews, persecuted by Christian Europe, sought refuge in the Muslim World. Not long ago, hundreds of thousands of them ran away from Spain when Ferdinand and Isabella, following their conquest of Granada in 1492, ordered all Jews and Muslims to be either baptised or put to the sword. Many more ran away when, having pretended conversion to Christianity, an "Inquisition" was arranged to expose their alleged "apostasy." All of them were received and accomodated with open heart and arms by Muslim North Africa. Some of them, travelled further east in the Muslim World in search of livelihood and fortune. Some landed in the midst of the Ottoman capital to become its financiers and tradesmen. Others rose to prominence to become viziers to the Sultan. More recently, numerous Jews from Western Europe, caught between Catholics fighting Protestants and vice versa, had equally found refuge in the Muslim World, in the Ottoman Empire perse. The Sultan therefore granted the request, and the first Jewish settlement was established in Neter, a few miles east of Yafa, and began to function as an agricultural station. Little did the Ottoman Government suspect what the future was to bring. The first Jewish settlement in Palestine was exclusivist from the start. It was meant to be, and it was in fact, a purely Jewish settlement.

Nothing happened between that incident and World War I. Zionism was trying desperately to convince the European Jews of its thesis. There was no need to convince them of the negative part of the Zionist thesis, namely, that Christian Europe was pre-eminently anti-Jewish and there is no hope of a change, the glaring facts of pogroms being still in memory. However, the Jews of Europe could not yet digest the positive side, namely, that they ought to uproot themselves and go elsewhere. And there was as yet no viable "elsewhere" to go except the new world. Zionism was in those days the sport of Jewish intellectualism in Europe. Zionist leadership was weaning itself away from Germany, and cultivating a new collaboration with the Allies, Britain and France.

B. The Balfour Declaration

World War I presented the breakthrough. Sharif Husayn, Ruler of the Hijaz and of the two holy cities, Makkah and Madinah, was a naïve simpleton with an air for self-deceiving grandeur. He was anxious to carve out an empire for himself and thought that World War I furnished a good opportunity. British intelligence approached him with a suggestion of an anti-Ottoman revolt and baited him with the promise that following Allied victory over the Ottoman Empire, the whole territory between Egypt and Iran would be his, united under his rule. At the same time, the Sykes-Picot agreement between Britain and France fragmented the territory into five segments, and assigned two of them to France and three to Britain. Britain, at still the same time, gave the Zionists the Balfour Declaration under which she committed her government to establish a national home for them in Palestine. It was the double-cross story of the century, European colonialism at its worst.

The Arab armies of Sharif Husayn and of his three sons, 'Alī, Faysal, and 'Abdullah, cleaned the area of Ottoman troops, to find themselves invaded by the British and French armies, who occupied the territory without let or hindrance. The Arab armies were forced to surrender their arms and disband. In the meantime, Sharif Husayn and his son 'Ali passed away. Fayşal was made nominal King of 'Iraq and 'Abdullah, a nominal Amir of the land beyond the Jordan River for which the name "Trans-Jordan" was invented. Syria and Lebanon became French protectorates; and Palestine, Trans-Jordan, and Iraq British mandated territories. The Sykes-Picot agreement was ratified by a resolution to this effect from the League of Nations in which Britain and France played the decisive role. President Hoover had withdrawn the United States in disgust over European wrangling and greed, over Britain and France's failure to honour their promises, or to respect the findings of the King - Crane Commission, an Anglo-American Committee sent to ascertain the desires of the natives of the same Arab lands in accordance with promises of democracy and self- determination made by the Allies. The end of the First World War thus found the Arabs of the "Near East" divided into five "states." The Hijaz had been conquered by the small army of 'Abd al 'Aziz, founder of the Kingdom of Su'ūdi Arabia, who emerged from Eastern Arabia after a silence of a century following the crushing defeat of the Wahhabi movement launched by Muhammad ibn Su'üd, 'Abd al 'Aziz's ancestor and Amir of Dar'iyyah, by an Egyptian army operating under the behest of Istanbul. While each of these "Mandate" states struggled under its newly imposed yoke of colonial occupation, the Hijaz and hinterland of the Arabian Peninsula was left for 'Abd al 'Aziz who depended upon the meagre income the annual pilgrimage brought. Further West, Egypt and the Sudan were under an older yoke of British colonial occupation. The same was true of the rest of North Africa which fell under French and Italian rule before the World War.

C. The British Mandate on Palestine

To return to Palestine. Palestine was a fertile land populated by about a million people practicing agriculture. The coastal plain had a good rainfall, a few small rivers, and water wells capable of irrigating a large stretch of the plain between Havta and Ghazzah. The Northern plain, Marj ibn 'Amir [Plain of Esdraelon], which runs from the Mediterranean to the Jordan River, was a rich alluvial land which produced cereals and fruits. The northern and central mountains were covered mainly with olive and some with fruit trees. The Jordan valley was rich with sun and water, tropical greenery of fruits and vegetables. Only the hills of Hebron and the Naqab desert around Bi'r al Sabi' were dry and poor by comparison, for their farming depended on rain which was scant. The land was divided into small farms worked out by all members of the family. Politically, the Palestinians regarded themselves as citizens of the larger Muslim World around them. Those of them who excelled would rise with the Ottoman hierarchy on a par with the citizens of any other part of the Empire.

Most of the Palestinians were Muslims. A few, about a fifth. were Christians, and about 1.5% were Jews. All spoke Arabic and belonged to Arab culture and civilization. Ethnically speaking, they were a mixed lot. For they descended from the original Canaanites and Philistines with a mixture of Hebrew. Greek, Persian, Roman, Arab, European-Crusader, Egyptian and Turkish blood. Palestine has known many regimes, but its people persisted through all of them. It has known many invasions all of which its people either repulsed or absorbed in time. Finally, Palestine has known numerous languages and cultures superseding one another throughout its history; but its people persisted throughout their succession. Indeed, they were the continuous human substrate which rejected and repulsed, or received and absorbed, enriched and fertilized, acculturated and converted the invaders, that gave Palestine its continuity in history. Nothing could be more spurious than the argument that because today's Palestinians are Arabs, they had gained possession of the land by conquest in 635 A. C. The Arabs have indeed conquered Palestine then; but they did not empty it of its native population and refilled it with manpower imported from

Arabia. The conquering Arabs intermarried with the natives, converted most of them to Islam, and all of them to Arabic language and culture. The Palestinians are as Canaanite, Philistine, Hebrew, Greek, and Roman as they are Arab. That the Arabs were the last to convert the Palestinians, does not alter the fact of their persistence through the centuries.

In thirty years of colonial administration, the British Government transformed Palestine into a country divided against itself. From 1918 to 1948 about 600,000 Jews from Europe were allowed to settle in Palestine. The Palestinians were in constant rebellion, with large explosions punctuating history every two or three years. The prisons and concentration camps were always full of Palestinians incarcerated for no crime but their rejection of the Zionist and colonialist policies of the British Government. That government was in every sense a police state built on overwhelming terror. Practically every one of the British heroes of World War II, from Wavell to Montgomery, had his training in Palestine, pursuing and killing Palestinians in rebellion against British Zionist policy.

The little over half a million Jews that entered Palestine settled in the most fertile plains. The overwhelming majority of them settled in the most fertile parts of the land, namely, the northern half of the Jordan Valley, Marj ibn 'Amir, and the coastal plain between Hayfa and Yafa. These parts of Palestine have always been under intensive agriculture for centuries as witnesses every report of every traveller, Western pilgrim or Muslim, since the Arab conquest. Contrary to the Zionists' claim that they were fulfilling the Isaiahn dream of making the desert bloom, they occupied no desert and made none bloom. In actual fact, they were ill adapted to the land's agricultural needs, applying new untested methods. Their agricultural settlements, whether the small holders variety or the

Kibbutz, were all running at a deficit all the time, from their foundation to the middle of World War II, when war time buying by the British and other armies in Palestine balanced their budgets. This is despite the fact that the land was paid for by the Keren Kayemet (The Jewish Agency) and Keren Hayesod (The Jewish National Fund) as were the capital investments in buildings, animal stock and equipment.

D. Zionist Acquisition of the Land

The lands on which these agricultural settlements stood amounted in 1948 to no more than 3% of Palestine. An infinitesimal portion of them was acquired directly by purchase from its Palestinian owners. The small and poor farmers who sold their lands to Jews had to balance their awakening consciousness of the national danger Zionism posed, against offers of purchase at ten and twenty times the normal value of the land. The Zionists bought the land with an eye on politics and colonisation rather than on economics, just as they picked out the site of the land with an eye on colonisation under military security, rather than finding a shelter from Europe or fructifying the desert.

The largest part of Jewish land acquisitions were made by other means, purchase from absentee landlords who never worked or lived on the land, and appropriation of state domain. Large tracts of land in the Hülah region (upper Jordan Valley) and Marj ibn 'Amir plain belonged by title to absentee Lebanese and Syrian landlords who led a life of debauchery in the European capitals. They had inherited their lands from powerful ancestors who at one time or another worked as tax farmers to the Sultan. In few cases, the land became theirs by a direct fief tendered by the Sultan for some service. In most others, they offered to pay the tax on behalf of the farmer- owner who in a year of drought or lack of means could not make the payment. Accumulation of tax debts soon brought the transfer of the land title to the tax farmer, often without even the knowledge of the farmer-owner who continued to live on and farm the land as before; and to give up part of his crops in taxes as before. What did it matter to him whether in a certain register in distant Istanbul, or nearer Damascus, which he had never seen anyway, his name or that of the tax-collector showed against the land? What did it matter whether the crops or cash he had to pay at harvest time was called "tax" or "rent?" It fluctuated anyway depending on the abundance of the crop. Thus, over the generations large tracts of land came to be owned by these landlords. Accustomed to high living, the disturbances of the World War and the continuous revolts against colonial occupation made their lives in the cities unbearable. Their agents continued to collect and deposit the incomes in the banks while they sought pleasure and comfort in Europe. The Zionists were quick to capitalise on the situation. Large sums of money were offered, and the transactions of sale concluded without the farmers on the land knowing anything about the matter.

The same was true of the rest of Jewish land acquisitions, namely state domain lands. Where the tax farmer was an honest official working for the government, or a poor functionary devoid of means with which to speculate, the same situation of failure to pay taxes would end up by a decision of a tax court passing the title to the land to the Sultan as chief of state, i.e. to the government. The same considerations obtained, the farmer-owner being unconcerned except for the immediate possession and cultivation of the land which he always continued to enjoy. In fact, the land registry title of the land was for him an esoteric affair. He not only lived on and cultivated the land exactly as if it were his real own, but he "sold," "rented," "divided" and disposed of the land between himself and his peers in the same or neighbouring village as if neither land registry, nor Istanbul, nor Sultan, nor tax-farmer or collector existed at all. The titles arising out of such transactions were kept in his turban or under his pillow; and they alone mattered. When the British set up their Mandate over Palestine, they, by one stroke of the pen, declared themselves heirs to the Ottoman Government and hence "owners" of the lands registered in the Sultan's name. These lands were henceforth called "state domain."

The absentee landlord was offered his millions in Paris and Rome. He sent an attorney to sign on his behalf in the new British Land Registry in Jerusalem. On the other hand, State Domain belonged to the government. The "government" was not only a colonial administration in whose eyes the local farmer meant little or nothing, but it was headed by a British High Commissioner who was himself a Zionist Jew, as in the case of Herbert Samuel, or a pro-Zionist Christian such as Arthur Wauchope and Harold MacMichael. Moreover, the very Mandate incorporated the Balfour Declaration. Hence, the "government" itself listed among its purposes that of establishing the Jews in Palestine and transforming it into a national home for them. The Jewish Agency had only to choose the lands it wished to acquire, in accordance with a militarily laid out plan of settlement of area after area, and the "government" would effect in the land registry the following typical scenario: The Keren Kayemeth's representative would apply for leasing the land in question for 99 years at the rate of one Palestinian Pound (at the time $4.00) per year per one hundred acres, and the "government" would agree and enter into the land registry the name of the lessee as possessor for the near-century duration. Constitutional reasons dictated that the government cannot sell its state domain land though officially it is the owner of it. Hence, the transaction took the form of a lease for 99 years. Any Western state constitution would enable a government to dispose of small portions of state domain in the interest of the public welfare. In this case, however, it was large port- ions of thousands and thousands of acres, the purpose being eventually to hand over the whole of the state domain lands to the Zionists. Anxious to maintain a foothold for themselves in Palestine unto eternity, the British thought a renewable lease for a century at a give-away price would fulfil the Zionist need just as well.

It was one thing to "buy" the land in Paris, or to "lease" it in Jerusalem, and another to take possession of it in the field. Since the farmer lived on the land, possession would not be effected without eviction of the Palestinian occupants. Such Palestinian land occupant was never even informed of what happened, and the eviction order always came to him as a surprise which he could not comprehend. Indeed, the surprise was always planned militarily. The Palestine Police Force - maintained with three quarters of the total state budget-would arrive at the scene at dawn with its cavalry and machine guns, as well as its trucks to transport away the farmer, his family and their miser- able belongings. Behind them would stand the Zionists, ready with their tractors to plough the land over whatever crops it contained, bulldozers to level whatever houses, shacks or tents stood on it, and group workers ready to fence the new acquisition with barbed wire. Behind the Zionists stood the British Army troops with their bayonets drawn, their mortars and guns on the ready, their armoured vehicles completely surrounding the whole area of action. All of a sudden, the Palestinian had to make the decision, with his children and family yards away, whether to resist and die or be uprooted from the land of his ancestors, the land on which he was born, the land which he has tilled all lifelong. In most cases where the farmers were few in number, the resistance ended with a beating with sticks and stones and a temporary arrest in jail. Where the number of farmers to be evicted was considerably larger, the resistance was always bloody. Tens of thousands of Palestinians laid down their lives against British bayonets drawn to effect the occupation of the land by the Zionist settlers from Europe.

E. Zionist Immigration to Palestine

At the beginning, the stream of Zionist immigrants to Palestine was a trickle. It was not until 1933, when Hitler assumed power in Germany and began his anti-Jewish campaigns, that the floodgates opened. Running for their lives, the Jews of Europe stampeded by all manner of means out of Christian Europe. Christian France, Britain and her great Empire, and the United States, with their immense territories and still more immense capacities for absorption of the Jewish refugees, closed their doors in their face. They too, though not as openly as Hitler, were anti-Jewish. Vociferously, they called on the Arabs to accept the Jewish refugees, but they would not accept them in their midst. These Christian benefactors must have thought that since there is another place, a distant Palestine where Jewish Zionist leadership wanted to take the Jewish refugees, then, Good Riddance! The argument that the Christians were laden with a guilt-complex because of their previous persecutions of the Jews, or of the repetition of such crimes by Christian Germany and Italy, or that they desired to fulfil the moral imperative of charity in helping the Jews to escape, is the most bogus argument of the century. In Christianity, moral contrition and atonement begin and end in the person, charity in the giving of his own self, his own wealth and property, not that of someone else. By giving in charity the stolen property of someone else, a property seized in the armed robbery that conquest by war is, the Christians of the West proved themselves as far from Christian morality as anyone can be.

The relatively few Zionist settlers that arrived in Palestine before 1933, and the relatively larger numbers which arrived thereafter, huddled together in their agricultural settlements, or in their urban quarters built on the edges of cities. Both were meant from the start to be exclusivist enclaves, closed, and segregated, totally Jewish, the purpose being, as the Zionist adage goes, "to make Palestine eventually as Jewish as Cromwell's England was English." The agricultural settlement was always surrounded with barbed wire to keep the Palestinians physically out. Not only was no Palestinian ever permitted to own or work any land within the settlement; he was never employed as labourer or allowed in as seller or customer. The Zionist agricultural settlement was literally out-of-bounds to the Palestinian who risked his life approaching its barbed wire fence. The trees in it may have been planted by himself or his parents or grandparents; but they were not his to touch, under pain of death by the bullet of the watchman at the bunker or turret a few yards away.

The urban settlement was not fenced with wire except during the violent disturbances which erupted so often everywhere. At other times, Palestinians were free to walk in the streets, to buy in the stores. But the stores, offices, and industries never hired a Palestinian to work in them. They never purchased anything from a Palestinian except in the direst of necessity. Their schools were absolutely closed in the face of Palestinian children. So were all their other public institutions and voluntary associations of all kinds. Only after 1948, did the Histadrut (General Federation of Labor) and the Communist party admit their first Palestinian member, obviously for political reasons alone. They sought to give themselves a semblance of democracy and pluralism. If the Jews had any contact with the Palestinians, it was with them as patients of their aggression, or as paying consumers of their goods and services.

F. Civil Inabilities of the Palestinians

The Palestinians could not act positively, whether in the economic or the political arena. Rebellion was the only road open to them. They were bereft of their right of association with one another by the British colonial government which decreed that no five adults could arrange a meeting of any sort without prior permission from the police; that no shop or business could be started without authority from the government; that no import or export of anything could be made without a licence; that in most areas, no travel or transportation from place to place could be done without government authority. The Palestinian who grew oranges for export, did in fact send his oranges to London, but he never sold them there. They were sold for him by agents of the Government, and he had to accept whatever proceeds were assigned. As export prices were fixed behind his back, so were the import prices of whatever commodities he needed. Jewish production was "protected" by insurmountable tariffs imposed by the government against competition from the outside, even if that outsider happened to be a British factory.

The Palestinian was never free to build a home or shop, or to raise any other building without governmental authority. The Government dispensed its authority to build lavishly on the Jews in their areas; and withheld it from Palestinians whose quarters, in consequence, became overcrowded and deteriorated gradually. Whereas the Jews began with a land free of buildings and planned their villages and cities in accordance with the most modern techniques, the Palestinian villages and cities were medieval and they could not change without an authority which the colonial government hardly ever gave. Worse yet, the town-planning councils, headed always by a British officer, included within the town-planning areas such agricultural land as the Zionist development plans called for, even if owned by Palestinians. The result was an immediate quadrupling or quintupling of taxes on the land, and the Palestinian owners had to sell or be dispossessed for failure to pay the new taxes.

From the start, the Jews established their own completely independent system of education. They were free to indoctrinate their children into Zionism, hatred, and contempt for the Palestinians, and even train them in paramilitary organizations, as they pleased. For military training, the British colonial administration supplied free armaments as well as manpower. Per contra, no Palestinian was allowed to open a school, the only schools other than government institutions allowed to function were the pre-elementary Qur'an and a few junior high schools run by the Muslim Supreme Council. The latter were no competition to the government schools built with public funds and whose graduates were readily employed as clerks by the colonial government. Missionary schools run by European powers or their missionary organizations were encouraged, but they were restricted to Palestinian children alone. Never was a Christian missionary school opened in a Jewish area for Jewish children. Evidently, their purpose was not to teach "Christ crucified" to humans, but to help alienate the Palestinians from their own tradition, and divide them into culturally disparate groups (French, Italian, German, Russian, American, as well as the various Christian Church denominations) which can never work for national homogeneity.

Whenever the Palestinians saw the need for a new school, they had to go to the colonial government to assess that need and plan for its satisfaction. The government imposed property taxes, poll taxes on the local inhabitants, as well as excise taxes on flour, sugar, tobacco, and other basic commodities. Only when such funds accumulating in the Government treasury rose to substantial amounts, did the Government move its public works department to design the school. This latter procrastinated as long as it could and then came out with plans which required years more of taxation to meet the costs of building. When finally, the building was completed and all the funds spent, the school stood empty, or was given one teacher when there was room for six, because there were no funds budgeted to operate it.

The Jews were always free to send their children to Europe for college and/or graduate study. They were allowed and encouraged to build several colleges in Tel Aviv, and the university in Jerusalem. Their financial resources seemed infinite. As to the Palestinians, their highest educational institution was the government high school; and the highest degree awarded was the London Matriculation. Their high school graduates were not free to go overseas for an education. Indeed, they were not free to travel to Beirut, Damascus, Baghdad or Cairo without a police permit which was rarely granted. Admission of Palestinians into any British university or college was in the hands of the colonial administration which did everything in its power to discourage and prevent it. Education in other European universities was in the hands of the missionary schools. Too poor to afford the expense of education overseas even if permission was granted, the Palestinians remained deprived of higher education, as if the duty of the mandatory government was to keep them in ignorance and backwardness. It was not until the mid-thirties that the one million Palestinians produced three or four B. A. graduates from England who took up duties as servants of the colonial administration upon their return home. Moreover, they were all sons of Palestinians who collaborated with the British Government.

The Zionists took complete advantage of the situation, the British being there precisely to help them do so. The Palestinians were systematically denied any help to the end of fulfilling the Zionist objectives, the British mandate having little else to aim at as far as its internal policy was concerned. The Jews quickly monopolised industry, the import-export trade, the professions, and the higher posts of the government. When World War II broke out, they moved immediately to monopolise and benefit from every activity associated with the "war effort."

G. The Palestinian's Continuous Rebellion

Despite all these attempts at keeping them down, backward and ignorant, at dividing and impoverishing them, dispossessing them of their land and inheritance, at isolating them from their Arab brothers to the North, East, and South, from world currents and developments, the Palestinians made remarkable advances. Above all, they sustained a continuous armed struggle against the might of the British Empire. Despite the fact that the Zionists were self-separatist and closed to every- thing native or Arab, they were not the target of these revolts which were aimed at the British exclusively. Throughout the British Mandate, the Palestinians undertook little or no action against the Zionists. Partly, they did not yet quite understand them, for they were absolutely strange and foreign, and little did they ever come into any significant contact with them. Partly, too, they understood only too well that the real villain was the British Government that had imposed upon them its administration and policy and brought these apparently help- less refugees in their midst.

The Palestinians' revolts were continuous, 1918 to 1948, with major outbreaks occurring every two to three years. Sporadic armed resistance took place in all districts, and the major outbreaks were universal and ever-increasing in intensity. Hundreds of thousands were killed on the streets of the cities, the highways, the open countryside, or were arrested and thrown in jails and concentration camps. The Government budget for all other services never exceeded one half of the budget for "Police and Prisons," as it was then called, not to mention the British army budget for Palestine operations which came out of the "Home Budget" of the United Kingdom itself. The revolt of 1938 exceeded all expectations. The whole of Palestine became a no-man's land. With the breakout of World War II, political leaders from other Arab countries pressured the Palestinians for an armistice, and the British Government for a settlement of the problem. The White Paper was issued by the Government in which it recognised that its Balfour Declaration had fulfilled its objective and that henceforth, there shall be neither immigration nor land transactions to Jews except with Palestinian approval. The Palestinians were only partly satisfied. They silenced their guns and returned to work to help once more the cause of freedom and democracy. As to the Zionists, though this was diametrically contrary to their ideals, their leadership had the bigger problem of the war to face. It pledged its support to the Allies' war effort and founded the Jewish Legion. During the war, thousands of Jewish escapees from Europe were given immigration certificates to Palestine as a war measure or were smuggled into the country.

H. United Nations Partition of Palestine

Following World War II, the Palestinians, as an integral part of the Arab World, were engulfed by a surging tide for general political liberation. For their part, the Zionists too began to agitate for repeal of the White Paper; and the situation in Palestine deteriorated on all fronts. Defying its provisions, the Zionist leadership began to force the way into Palestine for the Jewish refugees from Europe with arms. When Britain resisted their attempt in fear of evoking the Palestinians into renewing their armed struggle, Zionism opted for terrorism. The Haganah, the Stern Group, and the Irgun Zwvi Leumi, founded previously in secret, began operations designed to humiliate individual British administrators and force their hand.

Unable to sustain another military campaign and finding herself under mounting pressure from the United States to give in to the Zionist demands, Britain first resorted to the Anglo- American Committee to find a solution, and finally tossed the hot problem into the lap of the United Nations. President Harry Truman did not regard himself or his government bound by F. D. Roosevelt's commitment to King 'Abd al 'Aziz, that the United States of America will not support any solution of the Palestine Problem in which the Arabs had not been consulted and to which they did not agree. He openly supported the Zionist demand for immediate admission of 100,000 Jewish immigrants to Palestine, and thus for the repeal of the White Paper. He put the whole power and might of t of the United States of America behind the Zionist attempt to win a United

Nations resolution for partition of the country and the setting up of a Jewish State. Motivated by his Jewish partner from his haberdashery days, and flouting every advice of his own secretaries of state and defence, Harry Truman instructed the United States ambassadors around the world to exercise every pressure possible upon the governments to which they were delegated to vote for the partition plan. As soon as the vote was taken in favour of partition, Britain began a systematic pull out handing practically all their armaments to the Haganah. After 30 years of British Mandatory administration designed to prepare the natives for responsible independence and self-rule, the mandatory power left Palestine in a state of chaos with the majority of its people unable to protect themselves against the Zionist settler-invaders.

I. Emptying Palestine Through Terror

The Haganah and its shock troops, the Palmach, had been trained for years for this day. They pounced upon the unarmed Palestinian villagers and wiped out several of them prior to the official end of the Mandate on May 15, 1948. By their terror, their massive massacre of the innocent, of women and children, they caused the Palestinians to stampede, running away for their lives. In most cases, Jewish army trucks on the ready carried the Palestinians to their exile beyond the borders set, not by the Partition plan but by the Zionist leadership. For the plan to empty the largest possible area of Palestine of its native population was carefully laid out long before the events accompanying the birth of the Jewish state. The Zionist argument that the Palestinians sent themselves into temporary exile on the command of their leaders is pure rubbish. Human beings do not leave their homes, lands, personal belongings and effects, the country of their birth, on the command of anyone.

But when bombs fall all around, bullets buzz past the ears and a cruel enemy bent upon wholesale massacre approaches, then and only then one leaves; nay, one would then run and leave the door to his house wide open. These tactics had become popular during World War II. The Wehrmacht would concentrate all its power on one point in the line and demolish it so perfectly and completely that its example may be used to terrorise the other points and demoralise their defendants before the attack. Rommel obtained surrender from several Allied army posts in the Western Desert by reminding them of the massacre of Bir Hakim. So, the Zionists attacked the village of Deir Yasin, and literally wiped it out men, women, children, as well as animals and buildings. They then brandished the example before other villagers with the order to leave their homes and march. Through such terror-tactics, the Zionists obtained a portion of Palestine denuded of its native population. Palestinian lands, homes, furnishings - indeed Palestinian kitchens, bedrooms and dining rooms, all completely furnished and ready, received Jewish immigrants. This was the most massive armed robbery on the grandest scale, and with the most thoroughgoing results history may have witnessed. Bigger robberies may have taken place elsewhere, but not without destruction of the properties in process of seizing them, or destruction of their rightful owners. Here, the case was neat and simple: A living, ongoing population was forced to walk out of their homes without the time to pack a suitcase. On the border they were stripped clean of whatever valuables they carried on their bodies. Then, another population, just as cleanly devoid of personal effects, home furnishings, homes, and lands, walked right in and took possession of the emptied lands and houses.

The majority of incoming Jews were not Zionists. They too had been terrorised into a stampede to exit from their homes in the Arab World where they had lived in peace and harmony for centuries. The Zionist leadership needed them as materials for the new state and hence planned in every case a strategy suited to bring about their stampede. It planted explosives in their synagogues and market places; connived with corrupt Arab officials to allow incidents of aggression upon them by bands of plebeians hungry for booty; and it plotted with Arab kings and ministers of state to permit their exodus to take place. Besides filling the Palestinian homes emptied of their inhabitants with new citizens for the Jewish state, the exodus of Jews from Arab countries was desirable because it provided Zionism with an argument justifying the terrorisation of Palestinians out of their homes. Zionism is guilty of two terrorisations: that of emptying Palestine of its innocent and rightful owners, and that of uprooting Jews who are equally innocent and rightful owners of their homes in the Arab World.

It was to stop this operation of emptying and refilling that the Arab states found themselves compelled by their own peoples to intervene militarily in Palestine. As states, they could not intervene until the British Mandate was officially over, on May 15, 1948. By that time, an area of Palestine twice as large as that allotted to the Jewish State by the United Nations Partition Resolution had already been emptied and occupied by the Zionists. Even so, the Arab states did not "protect" except such areas as were already agreed upon in secret by the imperial powers that they may occupy. For in May, 1948, the Zionists were no military match for the Arabs whose armies were preponderantly bigger and mightier. The three most effective ones were the Arab Legion of Trans-Jordan, the army of 'Iraq and that of Egypt. The Arab Legion was officered by the British.

It won decisive victories over the Zionists in Jerusalem, its men occupied the offices of the Jewish Agency - the Government headquarters of Israel-but was ordered to with- draw by King 'Abdullah in agreement with a British-Jewish- Jordanian entente. The 'Iraqi Army did not fight a single battle in Palestine even when challenged by Zionist forces, its preordained role being merely to keep the main portions of Jinīn and Nablus sub-districts under Hashimi control (monarchies of 'Iraq and Jordan). Finally, the Egyptian army was betrayed by its own king and his minister of defence by giving it restrictive orders, cutting down its supplies, and providing it with faulty ammunition, bringing about its defeat by smaller and weaker Zionist forces.

Armistices were arranged by the superpowers and the United Nations machinery, which they dominated. Their purpose was to give time to the Zionist forces to receive arms from the communist world. Anxious to fish in troubled waters, the U.S.S.R. knew well that the waters of the Middle East would not be troubled if Zionism were prevented at this stage from planting a beachhead in the Arab World. For the first time, Western, Communist, and Zionist interests coincided, and Czechoslovakia was given green light to supply the Jewish state with the most sophisticated weaponry ever to enter the Near East. The Arab states, divided against them- selves and fearful of evil designs against one another, accepted the armistice and bickered among themselves. When the Zionists were ready, another push was made in all directions to seize and empty the Ramlah-Lydda district, the Naqab all the way to the Red Sea, and most of upper Galilee including the cities of Nazareth and Safad. In May and earlier, the Palestinians, the contingent of Muslim Brethren from Egypt and the Palestine Liberation Force, an army of volunteers under the generalship of Fawzi al Qawukji, a former hero of Palestinian anti-British resistance, were the only ones that fought continuously in Palestine to the second armistice in July, 1948. In numerous instances on the battle front, Palestinians were betrayed by the Arab States' armies with false promises of supplies in men and materials.

J. Zionism and Colonialism

Following the second armistice, the superpowers continued to reinforce the Jewish state with military supplies in fear of Arab recoupment of their forces. In October 1948, the Zionists launched an offensive against Egyptian positions in the South in order to complete their mastery over the Naqab. The Arabs of Africa were thus to be physically separated from those of Asia, and the Jewish state was to have a free highway from its centre to the Red Sea. Manning the Egyptian position at Fālūjah was a colonel by the name of Jamal 'Abd al Nāsir who saw his own men die because of faulty ammunition and lack of military supplies.

After their conquest of most of Palestine, the Zionists re-enacted the disturbance laws of the British Mandate under which Palestinians were deprived of their civil liberties, and any resistance from them could be met with indefinite imprisonment and torture, arbitrary deportation, imposition of collective fines, confiscation of property, and summary execution. They enacted laws under which they could expropriate the lands of Palestinians still living within the Jewish State and, at least ostensibly, supposed to be its citizens. Even all these were not enough. They resorted to outright ruse, as in the case of Kufr Bir'im whose villagers were invited by the Zionist army to withdraw to the hinterland in order not to fall within the range of fire and then set up civilian Jewish settlements in their lands and in their homes. Arab villages were wiped off the map; the Arab character of numerous towns was obliterated, and the towns transformed into Jewish cities.

The interests of Zionism coincided beautifully with the imperialist interests of France and England. Both these colonial powers were embroiled in a desperate fight with the Muslim natives of their colonies everywhere. To win over them, i.e., to perpetuate the occupation of their lands, the exploitation of their natural and human resources, the use of their strategic positions on the globe, the Muslims must be kept divided, their energies dissipated, their economies primitive, their populations demoralised, their forces demobilised, their leaderships corrupt and irresponsive to their national aspirations. In an age of global anti-colonialism, nothing fulfils all these desiderata better than the presence in the very midst of the Arab World which is the heart of Asia-Africa, of an alien state – Israel - that is militarily superior to all of the Arab states combined, and capable of draining away their energies by its continuing conflict with them. This role was cut to order for world Zionism. The Zionist state would like nothing better than a role in world affairs which guarantees its occupation of the land and expands it, strengthens its state to the point of invincibility, and nurtures the Jewish hatred of all non-Jews, the Jewish persecution complex, and Jewish racism on which Zionism had rested the whole being and existence of Jews in the age of romanticism.

Chapter IX: Islām and Judaism

A. Three Levels of Parity and Communion

The attitude of Islām to Judaism is governed by the first Islamic principle of "din al fitrah" (religio naturalis) under which the Jews, being human, are endowed by God with true religion, like all other humans. The nature of this innate religiosity is the capacity to recognise God as God-i.e., as Creator, as Lord and End of Creation - and to recognise His will as the ought-to-be of human endeavour. This principle imposes upon the Muslim to honour and respect the Jew as carrier of God's religion, no matter how different his conduct may be from that of the Muslim, or his culture from that of Islam. This principle is the ultimate base of Islam's humanism. It admits of no exception, its universalism being a priori and absolute. All men are by nature carriers of divine religion. Their capacity to recognise and acknowledge God and His law constitutes the religionist's sensus numinus, the philosopher's sensus communis, and Islām's din al fitrah. "Hold yourself true to the religion [Ur- Religion] like a Hanif [follower of true religion before Islâm]! That is the natural religion which God endowed to all mankind. There is no variation in this creation of God. That is the true and valuable religion!" (Qur'an 30:30). In second place, Islām's attitude is subject to the principle that the Jews, like any other people or nation, have been given revelation; that is, they have been sent one or more prophets to convey to them in their own tongue the message of God. "There is no people unto whom We have not sent a messenger to warn them. We have sent no messenger but to convey Our message to his people in their own tongue and to clarify it to them" (Qur'an 35:24; 14:4).

This message is essentially the same as all messages sent to other peoples, though it may have been different in its context and concrete prescriptions. The essence which is universal consists of God's existence and unity, and of man's obligation to serve Him by fulfilling His commandments which are the summum bonum. "We have sent no messenger but with the revelation that men are commanded to serve God, and to avoid evil" (Qur'an 16:36). If the revelation, or the accumulated tradition of revelations, is different from other revelations and traditions, the difference is not in the essential realm. In essence, all revelations are one, and the difference is "domestic", composable under the aegis of the universal essence common to all. Such essence is the content, the "what" of religion. But content must be translated into prescriptions for daily life, for the solution of living problems. Its figurisation is necessarily relative to time, place and other conditions. It may also change from revelation to revelation even within the same religious tradition. This principle enables Islām to distinguish between an original content of religion - the unchanging essence-and the cumulative tradition of its figurisations; in short, between Ur-Religion and the historical religious traditions. In accordance with this principle, the Jews are accorded the place of "religious relatives." They are acclaimed as possessors of revelations from the only God there is, the God of all; and their revelations are essentially the same as the revelation of Islām. It adds to the first principle of the Jews' being innately endowed with true religion, with the capacity to recognise God and His law, the historical fact that they have indeed received revelations from God giving them the true religion.

Islam's attitude to Judaism is subject, in third place, to the Qur'an's identification of the Jewish religious tradition with its own.

For the Muslim, Noah and Abraham, Jacob and Isaac, Joseph and Jonas. Moses and Aaron, David and Solomon, etc. are prophets of God, whose names may not be even mentioned without invoking God's blessing upon them. Their personal images are forever pure: Each representing one or more aspects of righteousness, piety, and virtue, and all of them absolutely true to the divine imperative of service and obedience to God. The Muslim regards these not merely as patriarchs and heroes, but as prophets of God, each of whom received revelation from God. It is on this basis that whatever was associated with these prophets in Palestine was honoured and preserved by the Muslims as their own. Indeed, the Muslims extended this Islamic religious recognition to a variety of sites associated with a number of Jewish personalities: Nabi (Prophet) Samuel (NE of Jaffa): Nabi Rūbin (Ruben, south of Jaffa); Maqam (grave of) Ibrahim (Hebron); Maqam Dawûd (David, E of Jerusalem), Maqam Sarah (N of Hebron), etc. Greatest of all honour was accorded by Islām to Jerusalem as the city of the Prophets of God which served as Qiblah (orientation in prayer) during the first fourteen years of the prophethood of Muham- mad (SAAW) in Makkah and Madinah. Moreover, the ascent of Muhammad (SAAW) to heaven had to come through Jerusalem, whose prophets made a tradition of which he was the last exponent. Islām saw itself as another moment, final and culminating, of the tradition of Jewish prophets. Its own Prophet, Muhammad (SAAW), Islām saw himself as standing in the same line of Jewish prophets. Thus, Islām was a continuation of that same tradition of the one true religion revealed by God to man.

B. One Mesopotamian origin

The original Semitic, or *Ur-Semitic*, religion was not a tradition which belonged exclusively to the Jews, but was common to the whole family of Semitic peoples. The version of that tradition embodied in the Old Testament is peculiar to the Jews since they have canonised it as scripture. Earlier Jews or Hebrews had that tradition as well as others which have not survived. Jewish dispersions since the Assyrian conquest in 722 B.C. must have caused some of these traditions to dissolve into those of other Semitic peoples, just as the citizens of Israel, the Northern Kingdom, had dissolved within the countryside surrounding them. There is more than sufficient evidence, internal to the Old Testament, to prove that other records of revelation existed which were either edited, reformed or lost by the generations. There is, in addition, ample evidence from Mesopotamian texts dating centuries and millennia before the earliest Hebrew texts, where variants of the Jewish revelations may be read. The pre-Islamic Hanifi tradition which regarded the religious tradition of Ibrahim to Jesus as the true religion of God, and with which the Prophet Muhammad (SAAW) identified his revelation, was certainly one of those variants living in the memory of Peninsula Arabs. Only thus may the problem of "borrowing" between the two religions be solved. That Islām "borrowed" from Judaism certain notions or traditions as Abraham Geiger, Abraham Katsch and C. C. Torrey have claimed with no little superficiality or temerity-is as true as the claim that Judaism had borrowed from the Mesopotamians those same notions and traditions. Ancient Near East stories of Creation, of Moses' birth and career, of Joseph and Job, of Noah and the Deluge, and the notions of the "Word of God," the "God of the Mountain," of the Covenant, the law, revelation, service of God, have all been derived from older Mesopotamian traditions. These studies equally point out that the Hebrews have indeed borrowed from the Canaanites their Hebrew language, priestly system, sacrificial ritual, temple worship, as well as their whole religious calendar of agricultural occasions; and from the Persians, their Paradise and Hell, the Day of Judgment, Messianism, sacramentalism, angelology and demonology, apocryphal vision of the end, soteriology, and eschatology. For the appearance of each of these notions or theories in the Jewish tradition is dated and can be shown to have occurred at or after the Jews' contact with those peoples.

We reject the notion of "borrowing" as superficial and simplistic. We do not deny interaction between the peoples concerned; but we maintain that what constitutes a religion is not the individual elements which may coincidentally or otherwise be found in other traditions, but the essence or structure in accordance with which all elements have been welded together into an integral whole. This essence is what makes Judaism itself unlike the religions with which it has had its contacts through the ages. It seems certain that both Judaism and Islām have common ancestry, an "Ur-Semitisch" tradition of religious ideas with which each of them identifies and from which each draws and interprets according to its own genius.

The foregoing analysis is the way a secular historical scholarship would follow to explain the communion of Judaism and Islām on one side, with the religions of ancient Mesopotamia, on the other. There is an easier, simpler and far more straight- forward explanation which is that of Islam. That is the fact that all religions, and in this special case, the Semitic family of religions, come from one source, namely God. There are differences of religious idiom between them, but no more, just as their languages constitute a family with varying idioms. This religious explanation is no less critical than the historical, geographic, anthropological, literary, and linguistic explanations given by Western scholarship. (For detailed comparative analysis see this author's Historical Atlas of the Religions of the World. New York, Macmillan, 1974, "The Ancient Near East," pp. 3ff.).

Certainly, there can be no greater sympathy than self-identification. Islām identified itself with Judaism and called unto the Jews in these words: "Say [O Prophet]: 'O People of the Book! Let us come together on a fair and noble principle common to both of us, never to worship or serve aught but God, never to associate any other being with Him, and never to take one another as Lords besides God" (Qur'an 3:64).

C. Islamic Critique of Judaism

It is an altogether different matter that Judaism has been subject to critique by Islām. Having acknowledged a Jewish religious tradition and identified itself with it, Islām could criticise from within, just as the Jewish prophets did. The object of criticism is never the religion of God, the revelation given to the prophets, but the historical recording or empirical texts claimed to be divine, and the actual practice of Jews in history. This very task, practically every Jewish Prophet from David to Malachi had assumed and fulfilled in much the same way as the Qur'anic revelation had done. The most remarkable feature of this criticism is that it is directed against man's work, man's tampering with the texts of revelation, man's personal, social, economic, and political conduct; and that it is all made in loyalty to God, to His revelation, His religion. It is a criticism of the Jews' religious practice in terms of the Jewish primordial religion. Islām never doubts the revealed status of the Torah. The Qur'an asserts: "It is We Who revealed the Torah. In it are guidance and light. By it the prophets of God render judgment to the Jews, and so do after them the rabbis and priests who have memorised the revelations of God and preserved their texts" (Qur'an 5:44).

Islām recognises that God has specially favoured the Jews. "O Banů Isra'il, Remember the blessing I have proffered upon you, the special favour I have shown you" (Qur'an 2:47, 122). But it understands this as fulfilment of a covenant between them and God, their part of which is to serve God and do the good works. The covenant grants to the Jews the rewards of children, land, prosperity and happiness, and imposes upon them worship of God, charity, justice and righteousness (Qur'an 5:12). The covenant equally stipulates that if the Jews fail to keep their part of the covenant, God will inflict upon them His punishment. Defeat, dispersion, suffering, and unhappiness would be their lot (Qur'an 3:112; 17:2-8). Islām knows nothing of the "Promise;" i.e. the doctrine that God bound Himself to love, bless and favour the Jews forever, regardless of whether they realise their part of the covenant, allegedly because they are His sons and daughters, whose evil conduct would not affect their status as His children (Deuteronomy 9:5-6; Hosea 11:8-9). Indeed, it regards such doc- trine as blasphemous, regardless whether the beneficiaries are Jews or Muslims. God's judgment is never arbitrary, never unjust, never not-due, not-earned by him upon whom it falls. The Jews do ascribe such arbitrariness to God in order to maintain their otherwise unjustifiable election. Judaism asserts that God chose Abraham and ordered him to leave his city and people and emigrate; but it gives no reason for the choice (Genesis 12:1). This election of Abraham is nowhere justified. It is asserted to be "in the flesh" (Genesis 17:10) and made to pass biologically to his descendants regardless of their piety or conduct (Isaiah 9:6; 63:1-16). The Qur'an was the first to proclaim Abraham's emigration as due to his conversion from the idolatry of his people to the true religion of God revealed to him, to their attempted persecution of him from which God saved him by miracle (Qur'an 21:51-73). Its narrative found its way to Jewish literature in the Middle Ages, especially in the Midrash Hagadol which was discovered in Yaman in the 18th century (For a detailed analysis of this question see this author's On Arabism: 'Urūbah and Religion. Amsterdam, Djambatan, 1962, pp. 22-28.).

Flowing from this arbitrary election is the Jews' description of God as their Father and themselves as His children. Islām condemns this as a threat to God's trascendence, along with Genesis' assertion of God's children, or bene ha Elohim, marrying the daughters of men (Genesis 6:2-4), and God being father to the Jews as well as to their kings (Samuel 7:14; Isaiah 9:6; Jeremiah 3:19, 31:9). The Qur'an says: "The Jews claim: 'We are the children of God and His favourite.' Say: 'Why then does He punish you for your sins? Rather, you are people to whom God is related as He is to any other people' [Qur'an 5:18]... If you do good, it will be reckoned for you; if you do evil, it will be reckoned against you.... Your deeds are your judgment. Whether you return to good or evil, thither We shall return in dealing with you" (Qur'an 17:6-8).

Islām further criticises the Jews for tampering with the texts of revelation and suffering the originals to be lost through neglect, edition and outright falsification (Qur'an 7:162; 2:41-42, 75, 79, 174; 4:46; 5:41). This criticism was the beginning of Biblical textual criticism, a discipline which has first grown in the hands of Muslim historians of religions such as Ibn Hazm, Shahristānī and others. This Qur'anic criticism was corroborated by later findings of the discipline; so much so, that the old belief in verbatim revelation of the present text of the Torah is no more held except by the naive and the unlearned.

The third major criticism Islām directs to the Jews is that of failing to live up to the norms and imperatives God had revealed to them. The language of such criticism is as strong as any the Jews had heard from their own prophets. "Those who were entrusted with the Torah but did not trust its imperatives, are like the donkey carrying a load of books (Qur'an 62:5) When the revelations were forsaken or forgotten, We saved those who prohibited evil and inflicted upon those who practiced injustice a severe punishment for their evil... We have dispersed them into groups all over the world. Some are righteous and others are not; and We have invested them with prosperity as well as hardship that they may reckon and return to Us. After them there came generations who paid lip service to the scripture, assuring themselves that God would nonetheless forgive them (7:165, 169) ... Certainly Moses brought forth the revelation; but the Jews took to calf worship and injustice. Many of them are illiterate, conjecturing about the revelation with little knowledge. Woe to them that rewrite the scripture with their own hands for a mean price and claim for their composition divine status. Whenever a prophet came to them with what is contrary to their desire, they took to pride, denouncing some and killing others, and saying we are a hard and stiff necked people." (Ibid. 2:92, 78-79, 87).

Evidently, Islam's criticism of Judaism was mixed. The Qur'anic pronouncements left ample room for charging the Jews with shirk (associationism) and bad practice, as well as crediting them with true monotheistic faith and moral practice. This is obviously the "golden mean" between a "boneless pluralism where anything goes" - i.e. an absolute cultural relativism where no moral or religious criticism is possible since every "blik" is sui generis, autonomous and may be judged only by its own premises - and an absolute dogmatism where only one view is tolerated, and every variation is declared heresy. If anything, the Islamic view is tilted in favour of Judaism in so far as the three factors discussed above are concerned, namely, natural (innate) religion, revealed religion through past prophecy, and declared identity of Islam with Judaism. These considerations prepared the ummah of Islām to write the most illustrious pages of history as far as religious tolerance on the practical level, and religious rational criticism on the theoretical, are concerned.

D. Islamic Critique of Jewish Practice

The groundwork for Islām's religious rational critique of Judaism was laid down in the revelations of the earlier Makkan period before any Muslim had anything to do with Jews. There were no Jews living permanently in Makkah. Those that visited the city were not allowed in the temple vicinity but had to stay outside in the suburbs, like other non-believers in Makkan religion. Such Jews possessed neither social, nor economic, nor political prestige in Makkah. If the Prophet had known or met any of them, their relation must have been purely of the theoretical kind, i.e. religious. The Prophet would have presented to them the religion of Islam which had been revealed to him that far and argued with them calling them to Islām. By the time of the Hijrah (622 A.C.) all of Islam's points against Judaism have been revealed.

Upon arrival in Madinah, the Prophet issued a declaration which served as the basis of the newborn Islamic polity. It is known as "the Covenant of Madinah." It defined the nature of the Islamic state, and the relation of its Muslims and non- Muslim citizens. In Madinah, the Jews were "clients" of the dominant Aws and Khasraj tribes. Some lived within the city and others in the outskirts; some practiced agriculture and others black smithery, jewellery and local trade. Being clients, they had no social or political clout in the life of the city which, at the time of the Hijrah, was already dominated by adherents to Islām in both tribes. Certainly the Jews were of no practical consequence to the Prophet, to his religion, or to the emerging ummah. Equally certain is the fact that as yet, the Prophet had no dealing whatever with them.

1. The Covenant of Madinah or Constitution of the Islamic State.

And yet, it was these very Jews that the Covenant of Madinah benefited. Ibn Hisham, the earliest biographer of the Prophet said: "The Apostle wrote a document concerning the Muhajirün (Makkan emigrants to Madinah) and the Ansär (Muslim natives of Madinah) in which the bonds of friendship and agreement were struck between them and the Muslims. By virtue of this covenant, the Jews were established and recognised in their religion and their properties, and their reciprocal obligations were defined... "This is a covenant from Muhammad, the Prophet of God, governing the relations between the believers and Muslims from Makkah and Madinah and those who followed, joined, and laboured with them. They are one ummah to the exclusion of all others. The Covenant of God is one. The least of the believers may give protection to a stranger, and it will be binding to all. The Jews who have followed us [and entered the peace] are entitled to equal treatment as well as assistance. They shall suffer no injustice and crime. The perpetrators of such acts prejudice themselves and their immediate relatives. The same rights and obligations belong to the Jews of Banů al Najjar, Banū al Härith, Banū Sāʿidah, Banu Jusham, Banu al Aws and Banů Tha'labah, except the aggressors and the criminals This covenant is against any party's treachery... If the Jews have clients, their clients will be as themselves. No person whatever may go out to war against anyone without the permission of Muhammad; and no one may be prevented from taking revenge for a wound. Whoever murders a person slays himself and his household, unless the murdered is himself a murderer, for God will accept this. The Jews must bear their expenses and the Muslims theirs; each party must come to the assistance of the other against any attack upon the parties of this covenant. Each shall advise and counsel the other for the good, rather than evil. No party may cheat its ally, and none may be responsible for a crime committed by an ally. Assistance belongs to the sufferer of injustice, not its perpetrator... Madinah shall be a sanctuary of peace for the peoples of this covenant, and the stranger shall be as his host - within its precincts... Any dispute or difference likely to disturb the peace shall be referred to God-May He be glorified! and to His Prophet Muhammad... God is witness unto the more pious and beneficent of the contents of this document. Neither the people of Quraysh nor their allies may be taken as allies by the parties of this covenant; these are bound to help one another against any attacker of Madinah. If the Jews are called by the Muslims to make peace with anyone and to maintain such peace, they must do so. The same obligation holds if the Muslims are called by the Jews to enter into peace, except in the case of those who fight a war for religion's sake.'

This covenant is protection against treachery. Every person is responsible for his own deeds. But no protection is here implied for the unjust or criminal. Whoever goes out to fight or stays behind, is safe within this city of Madinah, except the perpetrator of crime and injustice. God is the Protector of the righteous, of the pious. Muhammad is the Prophet of God'" (Ibn Hisham, Sirat Rasül Allah. Cairo: M. A. Subayh, 1383/ 1963. Volume I, pp. 349-351).

2. Pax Islamica: The new world-order

The Covenant of Madinah defined the construction of the Islamic State and established the Pax Islamica, a new social order. It made the two coterminous and gave them the potential to include the whole world. Pax Islāmica is a new world order built on peace, a peace built upon reason, whose guarantor is God Himself. Under this order, non-Muslims of the world may join the Muslim community as citizens of the Islamic State. Their religion, culture, social, economic and political institutions, and properties remain intact. Two things, however, they must renounce: War, against the New Order, and isolationism. Their entry into the covenant of peace with the New Order means the cessation of war by definition, unless it to be to defend it against attack. In case of attack upon any group within the Order, or upon any of its members, institutions, or properties, the whole Islamic Order is to rise like one man in its defence; for, "the peace of the believers" or the "Covenant of God," is indivisible.

Secondly, the New Order is universal. It is the duty of the Islamic state to extend it over the whole earth. As it reaches the boundary of another state or an autonomous religio-cultural group, it is its duty to invite that group or state to join. Its call cannot be rejected. Primarily, it is a call to peace; and to reject peace is tantamount to declaring war. Thirdly, it is a call for peaceful interchange on the religious, intellectual, and cultural levels between persons - Muslim and non-Muslim - who are citizens of the Islamic state and their counterparts in the neighboring state. Such interchange is the substance of freedom, the freedom to convince others of one's views as well as to be convinced of theirs. The Pax Islāmica was an attempt, as successful as it was noble, not only to "strike swords into ploughshares" but to follow up with pulling down the barriers that separate human minds and alienates their souls from and against one another. No "iron curtain" was to remain standing between members of the family of humankind. That religions and cultures will lose their relativism, their isolation, their island- particularism, as a result of such interaction is certain. But that is exactly what Islām came to achieve with its untiring rationalism and comprehensive universalism. The Arabs, its first carriers and the world around them, have suffered enough from the divisions and wars engendered by tribalism and provincialism. Too well have they known the nethermost depths of particularism. If, therefore, as a result of international, interreligious, and intercultural exchange, the religio-cultural or ethnic national groups will become more homogenous with humankind, that is just as it ought to be. The Pax Islāmica was a "United Nations" fourteen centuries ago, and a far more effective and beneficial one than our contemporary world institution.

The Muslim did not give up his duty to call the Jews to Islām. But his call was to be conducted "with wisdom and comely presentation" (Qur'an 16:125). Under no case whatever may any human be coerced, or pressured, to change his convictions. "No coercion in Religion. Truth and Error are manifest. Whoever wishes to accept the faith may do so of his own accord and will to his own personal credit. Whoever does not, may do so to his own personal discredit [with God] (Qur'an 2:256). Throughout his life, and long after the establishment of the new World Order, the Prophet never tired of arguing out the matters of the faith with non-Muslims and Muslims alike, seeing to convince the former, and to clarify or deepen the conviction of the latter. Naturally, the non-Muslims were not only free to present their case, but were invited to do so. As natural and rational religion - non-sacramental, demythologised, humanistic, and critical faith in the unity of God, unity of truth, and primacy of the moral law - Islam has nothing to hide, nothing to lose and every argument to win.

The *Pax Islamica* embodied in the Covenant of Madinah transformed the Jews of Arabia, most of whom lived in and around Madinah and were signatories of the Covenant. From being *mawālī* or "clients" of a certain Arab tribe or another, enjoying the wretched status of an untouchable pariah yet bound to fight the tribe's senseless wars against other tribes, they became fully enfranchised citizens of a vigorous world-state. The Covenant conferred upon them the dignity of full membership in the new World Order. They stood no more under the arbitrary jurisdiction of their master tribesmen regarding everything they do, including the practice of their faith. Now they have become free. Their faith, culture and institutions are no more merely tolerated, or on sufferance, but dejure. Their responsibility is directly to the world state, and on the highest level. Henceforth, they are no more restricted or bound to the tribal territory or service, but free to go anywhere within the state, to serve or interact in peace with anyone. In short, the Covenant of Madinah made them universal citizens, free to contend among all men, to convince and be convinced. That is what Islām granted to them. As far as the Torah, or Jewish Law, is concerned, Islām recognised the Jews' observance of it not only as legitimate, but as desirable and obligatory to Jews for the continuation of group life under the constitution. The Jews were required to set up their own law courts, to judge themselves by the precepts of the Torah. Indeed, since under the Pax Islāmica man was defined by his religious affiliation, Judaism and its law got significant support from the Jews. For, under the New Order, they were not free to flout the Torah, as long as they adhered to the Jewish identity. Atheistic secularism, religious rebellion, withdrawal from the Jewish ummah without joining another Ummah, were not possible options for them, just as they were not possible for Muslims, nor for Christians. Assimilation and its dangers, above all, dilution of Judaism, relaxation or non-observance of its law, and its diminution through internal rebellion against the authority of its rabbinic courts, were removed once and for all. Equally removed were persecution and its consequences of self-enclosure and isolationism, of hatred and resentment, of immobility and deadly lethargy. For the Jews were as the Qur'an called them, "People of the Book" or Scripture, or revealed religion, who have entered the Covenant of the Prophet. Their guarantor was the guarantor of the covenant, viz., God Himself. In deference to that divine guarantee, the Prophet counselled: "Whoever commits an injustice against a Dhimmi [i.e., a member of the non-Muslim peoples of the Covenant of Madīnah) I shall be his prosecutor on the Day of Judgement.'

Here was a system under which the Jew could be a Jew, develop and maintain his institutions according to his own genius, not only legitimately, but with the active support of the state under its own constitution and culture. The oldest and deepest expectation, the most persistent hope of the Jew since the Babylonian Exile, was realised at last. For over a millennium, the Jew was not free to be a Jew. His Jewishness, in the eyes of Christianity, was an abomination which could be met either with proselitisation and conversion, or persecution. In the eyes of Islam, the Jewishness of the Jew was a temporary domestic deviation from one and the same primordial religion of God, which could be met only with a free exchange of rational and objective argument. Even as it stood in history, it is to be honoured and respected. Its adherents are to be encouraged and supported to practice it, and they ought to be protected in their observance of it. As long as they adhere to it, they are entitled to their corporate existence as a people under the constitution of the world state. This title was a title to freedom, legitimacy, protection and dignity in a universal order. Henceforth, the Jew may proclaim and worship his God wherever the banner of Islam was to be raised. His Exile, his status as an outlaw, have come to an end. Henceforth he is a Jewish citizen of the new World Order.

3. Political Treason by the Jews of Madinah

Unfortunately, the Jews of Madinah did not have the vision necessary for rising to the new dawn Islām has opened before them. Although they agreed to and ostensibly committed themselves to the Covenant of Madinah, they did not enter into it wholeheartedly. From the beginning, some of their leaders began to plot against the new Order, even as they paid lip service to it. Two years had scarcely passed when, seizing the opportunity of a military relapse of the Muslims at the Battle of Uhud and other lesser encounters with the Makkans, they entered into open challenge. With the bigger threats of Makkah on his mind, the Prophet confronted the guilty clars or houses -not the Jews as a whole-and forced them to leave the state. He hoped the Jewish majority which was not involved would honour the Covenant and remain true to the new Order. In the same year, another Jewish clan was caught plotting to murder the Prophet. It was meted out the same judgment of banishment and a new appeal was made to the rest to honour their part of the Covenant. A year later, after the Battle of the Ditch in which the inner defences of Madinah nearly succumbed in face of the onslaught of a tremendous alliance of Arab tribes with Makkah, in which the Jews played a treacherous role, the Muslims had no choice but to charge them with high treason. Many were executed in the process, after an arbitrator whom they had accepted had pronounced judgment against them.

The Prophet sought no quarrel with them. The Covenant of Madinah invoked God as its Guarantor, and this was confirmed in revelation. The Covenant was already a working constitution. Islam had previously voiced all its critique of Judaism as a religion and culture, and most of the Jews had not converted to Islam. For over two years, these Jews had practiced their faith in freedom and dignity. Their political behaviour, however, was a different and very grave matter. That is why the judgments pronounced against them varied proportionately to the gravity of the danger to which their plotting exposed the Islamic polity: Banishment with permission to carry their wealth away in the first case; in the second, banishment without such permission; in the third, execution of the able-bodied males convicted of high treason. The Judgments had ipso facto nothing to do with Judaism, the religion. Others, Muslim and non-Muslim, have been guilty of similar crimes and received the same judgment. That is also why, following the death of the Prophet, when the Jews who were banished from Madinah and settled in the North came once more under Islamic dominion, the precepts of the Covenant of Madinah were reapplied as if nothing had happened before.

E. The Golden Age of Judaism and the Jews

The same precepts governed the relations of the Jews of the conquered territories as soon as their Islamic administrations were set up. Until the last two or three centuries, the majority of world Jewry was still living within the Muslim World and was still prospering under those self-same precepts. Nowhere has Judaism ever found a haven as sympathetic and protective. Even in its days of Davidic and Solomonic glory in Palestine, a period which lasted less than two generations (c. 1000-922 B.C.), Judaism or whatever version of it existed, could be practiced only in the territory of its own state. Outside that territory, in the wide world, it was an abomination from the days of Jacob (following the racist Jewish attack against Schechem by Jacob and his sons and clan, according to Genesis 34). Even the Davidic state itself was the object of hatred and resentment within as well as without its boundaries, which awaited the day of its dissolution on 922 B. C. Internally as well as externally, the issue was the religion itself, the temple, its priesthood and the rituals of worship. For the first time in Jewish history, Judaism was practiced under the aegis of Islām without political, military, or subversive threat from any quarter. If it was threatened in any sense, it was so by reason of the appeal of a rationalistic humanism and universalism. But this is no threat at all. It is only an invitation to religious health, to religious growth, to religious clarity and felicity.

Throughout Muslim history, Judaism prospered more than it ever did before or outside that history. At no time was the Hebrew language spoken more widely or more correctly. The fact that the dominant language of Islam was another Semitic language, viz., Arabic, and the fact that it was known to the majority of Jews living within the Muslim World, helped the Hebrew speaking Jews to pull their language from the certain doom of pollution and corruption back to its classical roots in the Torah and Talmud. The classicism of Arabic moved the Jews to a similar classicism in Hebrew. Hence, no "Yiddish," "Ladino" or other vulgarisations of Hebrew took place under Arabic influence; and Hebrew poetry, prose and letters attained heights never attained before except perhaps by the

Biblical redactor. On the contrary. The Jews' knowledge of Arabic prompted their scholars to develop a Hebrew grammar, and to do so in a manner comparable to the grammar of Arabic, the language which properly served as prototype of all Semitic languages. This was accomplished by Abū Zakariyya Yahya ibn Dawūd in Cordoba in the last decade of the Fourth Century A.H./Tenth Century A.C.

Besides the flowering in the sciences of language and the arts of the pen, Judaism scored under Islām the highest development of its culture, on the level of ideas. For the first time, it achieved a systematisation of itself. Having been brought up in the most sophisticated milieu of the world, that of Cordoba, Mūsā Abū 'Imran ibn Maymün (1135-1177) produced his Dalālah al Ha'irin (Guide of the Perplexed) in Arabic, after mastering all the religious thought of the Hebrew, Christian and Islāmic religious traditions. He gave Judaism its first and greatest conceptualisation, relating its law, theology, and ethics together, and basing their ideational structure on rational logic and metaphysics. His systematisation remains the definitive statement of Judaism, and his formulation of the creed the dominant statement of the Jewish faith to this day.

Out of the religious atmosphere and cultural milieu Islām provided, came the two main currents of thought which divided the Jewish spiritual stream since then: The rationalist or legalist, and the mystical. The former was founded by Ibn Maymün himself; the latter, by Sulayman ibn Gabirol, 1021- 1058, whose *Yanbü' al Hayat* (Fons Vitae), also written in Arabic, introduced mysticism into Judaism. Ibn Gabirol was the source of inspiration for all Jewish mystical movements in the Middle Ages. His spiritualism helped the Jews of Europe bear their terrible suffering at the hands of Christians, and his writings were more popular among them than among their co- religionists in the Muslim World who, in absence of the disease, stood in no need for the cure. The Zohar, which dominated the spirituality of Europe's Jews, was a direct offspring of this trend introduced by Ibn Gabirol; while Karo's Shulhan Arukh was a European over-simplification of the systematised arrangement of the Torah by Ibn Maymün. These two works, together with the creed of Ibn Maymün characterised, oriented, and dominated the religious and spiritual life of European Jewry, while the works of Ibn Maymün alone did the same to the Jews of the Muslim World.

It cannot be denied that in modern times, the Jews of Europe and America have tremendous achievements to their credit in all fields of human endeavour - except religion. They may well have rivalled their Muslim World ancestors in the worldly sciences and the earthly glories. But it cannot be denied, either, that all these Jewish achievements of modern times have been realised at the cost of Judaism - the religion. For the spirit driving the age and milieu in which they were achieved was irreligious. It was born out of the struggle of the human mind to liberate itself from the naiveté of a dogmatic Church. The Western struggle against the Church, Biblical archaeology and criticism, the rise of the natural sciences, the growth of European particularism and ethnocentrism - all those factors dictated an orientation inimical to religiosity and transcendence, to the essence of the Semitic soul. Hence, the reduction of Christianity's determining power of social, political, cultural life of Western Christendom. More important and basic is the corrosive influence of all these forces upon the religion of Christianity.

The Jews' contributions to Western civilisation and culture may be truly great, but they are not Jewish. In no case may any of them be claimed as Jewish; i.e., conceived in loyalty to Judaism and meant as a positive expression of its being. Laments sung in loyalty to Judaism there certainly were; but these are neither great, nor may they be regarded as positive expression of Judaism in the sense that the Biblical statements, the Talmud and Midrashim, and the Maimonidean crystallisation were. Significant in this regard is the public debate which took place four years ago when New York City witnessed the opening of a "Jewish Museum" whose collections of works of art by Western Jews were declared by the better minds of Western Jewry non-Jewish despite their Jewish authors.

Islām, it must be said in conclusion, is "the best friend Judaism has ever had." It recognised Judaism as religion de jure, which no other religion or political system ever did. It not only tolerated the observance of the Torah but demanded it; and it placed its executive power at the disposal of the rabbinic court. In this, Islām has gone farther than the Jews' fondest diaspora dream. Per contra, in the United States of America, supposed by most to be the ideal prototype of tolerance, any application. of Jewish law where it differs from positive, secular, law would immediately land the parties concerned in court as violators of American law. Indeed, Islām was more friendly to Judaism than the Davidic-Solomonic State itself. Unlike that state which was born in conflict and perished seventy-eight years later in conflict, the Pax Islamica or World Order of Islam, which lasted fourteen centuries so far, covered half the world, and is still growing, provided Judaism with a world-stage in which to contend for men's minds, and a general respect for and loyalty to religion without which neither the religion of the majority nor that of the minority could prosper.

It is remarkable that Christian tolerance of the Jews came only as Christians lost their religiosity, whereas Islamic tolerance of them came as Islām dominated the life of its adherents. The ascendancy of Islām promoted respect for religion, any religion, anywhere; and thus provided a world atmosphere in which the Jew's claim to Jewishness, his loyalty to the religion of Judaism without which he is nothing, could be respected and honoured. It is surprising that the contemporary resurgence of Judaism is taking place in the age of secularism, under the dominion of the West which stands today at the zenith of anti- religious sentiment. *In hoc signo* is the evidence that the so- called resurgence of Judaism is no religious resurgence at all; and that Judaism has fallen easy prey and become a football in the hands of a secularist West which tosses it around for its own political ulterior motives.

Chapter X:
Islām and Zionism

A. The Injustice of Zionism against Non-Jews

What is the position of Islam concerning Zionism, the politics, the faith, and their achievements to date?

We have seen that Zionism, the politics, is an exercise in political power, designed to transform Palestine and its adjacent territories into a Jewish state, "as Jewish as England is English." Zionism's pursuit of this objective is thoroughly Machiavellian. Its single-minded purpose is given absolute priority over all considerations, including the moral. Prior to 1948, it sought to fulfil its purpose first by bribing and then by threatening the Sultan of the Ottoman State of which Palestine was a part. When this failed, it began to work for the destruction of the Ottoman State and put its forces at the service of its enemies.

The prime enemy of the Ottoman State was the British Empire. Zionism deployed all its powers - financial through Baron de Rothschild, and strategic science through Chaim Weizman to extract from the British Government the Balfour Declaration in which the British Government pledged its support to the Zionist cause, though it had already pledged to the Arabs freedom and unity of all territories evacuated by the Ottoman forces.

Having obtained the Balfour Declaration, Zionism played its power to the hilt to acquire land. It stopped at nothing in this effort, including the application of pressure, blackmail, bribery, speculation and, as we have seen, forced eviction of Palestinian farmers from lands which they had inherited from their ancestors through the millennia. Zionism wanted the land at any price; but by 1948, it got about 3% of Palestine through all means moral and immoral. Equally, Zionism sought to extract the Jews of Europe and settle them in Palestine. To this end, it used indoctrination and bargained with fascist and other governments. Its strategy was not to save all Jewish lives, but only those that could serve its purpose of military occupation and agricultural colonisation of Palestine.

It was after 1948 that Zionism uncovered its nature and began to operate in the open. Its plan was to empty Palestine of its native inhabitants and to occupy their lands, farms, homes, and all movable properties. In so doing, Zionism was guilty of naked robbery by force of arms; of wanton, indiscriminate slaughter of men, women, and children; of destruction of men's lives and properties. In order to obtain the human resources necessary to complete the plan, Zionism undermined the Jewish communities of the whole world. In the Arab World, where uprooting the Jewish communities would provide argument presenting the emptying of Palestine of its inhabitants as one half of a "population exchange, "Zionist action was brutal. Zionism terrorised Arab Jews by bombing their synagogues, destroying their businesses and assassinating their questioning or reluctant leaders. In its occupation of Palestine since 1948, Zionism has perpetrated immeasurable injustice against the Palestinians who survived its onslaught and remained in their homes. Internationally, the Zionist State has, since its establishment in 1948, terrorised the whole region, massacred the innocent by the thousands, destroyed innumerable villages, and drained the resources and energies of a whole generation of a hundred million awakening Arabs on futile wars which it imposed upon them.

B. Undoing the Injustice against Non-Jews

For this long list of crimes against the individual Palestinian men and women, against the corporate existence of the Palestinians, against the individual Arabs of the surrounding countries as well as the ummah, Islam condemns Zionism. Islām demands that every atom's weight of injustice perpetrated against the innocent be undone. Hence, it imposes upon all Muslims the world over to rise like one man to put an end to injustice and to reinstate its sufferers in their lands, homes, and properties. The illegitimate use of every movable or immovable property by the Zionists since the British occupation of the land will have to be paid for and compensated. Therefore, the Islamic position leaves no chance for the Zionist State but to be dismantled and destroyed, and its wealth confiscated to pay off its liabilities. This obligation to repel, stop and undo injustice, is a corporate religious obligation (fard kifayah) on the ummah, and a personal religious obligation (fard 'ayn) on every able adult Muslim man or woman in the world until the ummah has officially assumed responsibility for its implementation. Defense of the ummah, i.e., of every province over which the banner of the Islamic State has once been raised, is jihād, or holy war, and it is a prime religious duty. Fulfilment of this duty is falah (felicity) in this world and the next, i.e., victory in this world, martyrdom, and paradise in the other (Qur'an 3:169). Moreover, God commands the Muslims "to avail themselves of all means and instruments of force in order to overwhelm the enemy and bring the war to a quick end (Qur'an 8:60).

However, dismantling the Zionist State does not necessarily mean the destruction of Jewish lives or of properties. Such destruction will, however, be regarded by Islām as a necessary evil in case Zionist forces resist the dismantling and seizing process. It is a first Islamic principle that aggression and injustice be met with an identical proportion of same (Qur'an 2:194). Excess is absolutely forbidden. Moreover, hostilities must, according to Islām, be immediately stopped as soon as resistance stops. To continue them beyond acquiescence of the resistant is unpardonable injustice (Qur'an 8:61; 5:90). Islām commands the Muslims never to transgress, never to go beyond the termination of injustice, never to give vent to any resentment by increasing the suffering one atom's weight, but to deal to the enemy exactly what he had dealt them, measure for measure (Qur'ân 5:45). Islām equally commands its adherents to spare no effort, no matériel, no wealth needed to bring the war to victorious conclusion. It lays no time limit on the declaration or conduct of the war; for a moral religious obligation is ex hypothesis timeless. Islām further recommends pardon, mercy, and forgiveness (Ibid.). But these virtues cannot be forced; and they have moral value only if they are practiced from a position of strength and self-sufficiency. Moreover, they are strictly personal. They must be the object of a personal decision on the part of a free personal subject for them to be the moral value they purport themselves to be.

The injustice perpetrated by Zionism is so complex, so compounded and so grave that there is practically no means of stopping or undoing it without a violent war in which the Zionist army, state and all its public institutions would have to be destroyed. Even if the Western world forsook the Zionist State altogether, its Zionist leadership would still muster enough desperate courage to persist. For it is, by nature, an ideological state, necessarily prepared to save itself at all costs to human life and property. All the more reason, therefore, for the Muslims of the world to take it more seriously, and to prepare realistic plans which they are unquestionably capable of executing.

C. De- Zionization

Once the Zionist State, its army and other public institutions are destroyed, the problem of what to do with its population would have to be faced. That Islâm cannot and will not com- promise on Zionism is a lesson which must be taught to every Jew living in the Muslim World. Hence, Islām will not tolerate the establishment of a Zionist alternative to the Zionist State. All Zionists who wish to live within the Muslim World would have to de-Zionise themselves, emigrate, or face prosecution for their Zionist activities. De-Zionisation, it must be borne in mind, is the rejection of Zionism, the political program to transform Palestine into a Jewish state on the European or Western model.

Islām's unequivocal condemnation of Zionism is not restricted to it as a political program in which individuals were unjustly dispossessed of their personal properties. It goes beyond even the corporate Palestinian existence which the Zionist State has destroyed in its aggression, and which exacerbates its crime and responsibility. The condemnation in fact extends to the realm of thought and emotion. For, even if the injustice against the Palestinians were to be terminated and the Palestinians were to be adequately compensated for their damages incurred since the Balfour Declaration, Islām still would condemn a Zionist program whose object is not Palestine, but some non-Muslim corner of the world. Indeed, Islām will condemn a Zionist State even if it were set up on an isolated island or on the other side of the moon.

The cause of Islam is universal. The truth and value which God granted through Islām is meant for all mankind, not merely for the Arabs, the Semites, or the Asians. The moral and religious imperatives deriving from the Islamic revelation are valid - and hence, obligatory - for all men. The most basic of these, which are the other side of tawhid, or unisation of God, and are hence inseparable from it, are the egalitarian creatureliness of all men before God, their universal obligation to do justice, and their innate, personal and inalienable right to hear the word of God. Whether or not they are convinced by it is their own individual decision which may not be made for them, ultimately, by any ruler or government. Any violation of these first principles is a defiance of God, an attack upon His unity, transcendence and ultimacy.

D. The Injustice of Zionism against Judaism

Firstly, Zionism interprets Judaism in accordance with a preconceived stand of European romanticism based on arbitrary feeling. It understands God's election of the Jews as racist superiority over all God's creatures, and His covenant as irrevocable promise to His children whom it ambivalently understands in biological and spiritual terms by referring to it as being "in the flesh" and independent of moral conduct. This is discrimination among God's creatures in so far as they are His creatures. Such discrimination is a reflection on God's nature; for the first and essential definition of God is that He is the Creator of all. Zionism redefines God as the Creator of all men in one way, but the Creator of the Jews in another special way. This characterisation reduces the Godliness of God, i.e., His unity and transcendence, because it distinguishes contradictory defining characteristics in His essence. Thus, Zionism is an attack upon divine transcendence. This error, this blind judgment which Zionism accepts absolutely and bases its whole life- and world-perspective on it, leads its adherent to a life of moral casuistry and turpitude. The very same cause led Nazi Germany first to extend its domain so as to have an empire. For there is no sense to racist superiority if there are no other races over whom to exercise that superiority, just as expansionist Israel has been seeking to do during its thirty years of history.

Secondly, racist discrimination of Nazi Germany led it to commit untold injustice against those of its own citizens, as well as those citizens of other nations who fell under her sway, who do not fulfil the requirements of racist superiority as the standard bearers of Nazism defined it. The "Holocaust" of Jews, Poles, Slavs, and numerous others followed with logical necessity once the premises of German racism were postulated. Likewise, the Zionist State has reduced its non-Jewish citizens to second status; confiscated their lands and properties; subjected them to martial rule; jailed, banished or executed them without process of law - all in the name of Jewish racist purity and Zionist political ideals. Regardless of whether these unhappy humans were Arabs or non-Arabs, Christian or Muslim, the discrimination is against them as goyim, i.e., as non-Jewish humans. Indeed, the children of mixed marriages where the mother is non-Jewish have been subject to the same discrimination in the Zionist State, recalling what a racist redactor had reported about an earlier occurrence of racist dis- crimination and disowning of legitimate wives and children (Ezra 10:10ff; Nehemiah 10:28-30). Being directed against humanity at large, racist discrimination is a sin, an injustice, of which Zionism is guilty on a large scale. Islām binds its adherents to rise against injustice wherever, whenever, by whomsoever and against whomsoever it is committed.

Thirdly, no racist regime can maintain itself without setting up an iron curtain around it. Its ideology cannot withstand alternatives, for it is arbitrary and dogmatic. Its adherents are necessarily single-minded and bent on intolerance of other views. It does not make its claim rationally - i.e., with evidence and in openness to further evidence - but doggedly on a "take it or leave it," or "if you are not with us you are against us" basis. That is why the Zionist State has been a police state in every sense of the term, placing those of its citizens who do not share its ideology in a category which amounts to a large concentration camp if they are goyim, and under special supervision if they are Jews. That is also why no man, Jew or goy, may settle in the Zionist State unless he adheres to Zionism's racist ideology. Differences of opinion with the ruling ideology may be tolerated to mislead the outside observer into thinking the state to be a free, democratic one. But such differences can only be those which refer either to strategy or incidentals, never to basics. The very thesis of Zionism cannot ever be put to question by those who dwell under its dominion. The policy of a Zionist state must therefore be isolationist, shutting its people off from the word of God which challenges its essential doctrine.

E. Undoing the Injustice against Judaism

Islām demands of its adherents and institutions to make the word of God known to all humankind. It recognizes no state authority which shuts off a people from hearing the word of God. True, Islām can only present the word of God and cannot force its acceptance. But when the presentation of the word of God is itself prohibited or proscribed, the Islamic state is obliged to confront the prohibiting authority and break it up. For, the shutting off of any ear other than one's personal own is a grave injustice, a sin committed not only against the person who is object of it, but against humanity, and ultimately against God. Just as the conscience of humanity would be aroused to condemn a regime bent deliberately upon starving its citizens to death, the conscience of Islam is aroused to condemn, and demand action against, a regime bent upon starving the souls of its citizens, upon de-sensitising them to rational evidence, to moral and religious obligation - in short, to deface and dehumanise them as creatures of God.

It is not therefore beyond the jurisdiction of the Islamic State to transcend its own frontiers and to wage jihad or holy war against such Zionist State wherever it may set up its house to imprison its adherents therein. This obligation derives from the very nature of the moral law. Holding the moral law to be universal, based upon a primary sense of value that is innate to all humans as well as upon reason, the accumulated wisdom of mankind, Islām regards any restriction of the universal validity of the moral law as contrary to the nature of morality. Certainly, some restrictions of some moral laws are valid and permissible if they are made in the interest of realising higher moral laws. Such restriction is always rational, critical, open to contrary evidence, and supported by the cumulative moral wisdom of mankind. When the restriction is arbitrary, dogged, based upon "feeling" or "romantic experience" and running against the very grain of moral wisdom, it must not be valid. Charity and love of neighbour demand that what the moral subject has found to be the summum bonum be communicated by him to all other humans. If it is a sin deliberately not to inform one's neighbour in an apartment house of a fire in the building, it must be a sin a fortiori, deliberately not to communicate to him the summum bonum, the ultimate meaning of human life and man's destiny in eternal bliss or fire.

If, contrary to its nature, the Zionist State were to open its frontiers and permit its citizens to be exposed to the word of God, then the Islamic State can take no further action against it. The Islamic obligation to undo injustice cannot go beyond the penetration of the domain of injustice and the presentation to its sufferers and perpetrators with the alternative of morality and justice. This is the meaning of the Qur'anic verses: "No coercion in religion. The Prophet's duty is limited to communicating the message clearly; etc. (Qur'an 2:256; 5:102; 13:42; 16:82; etc.). It does not imply a toleration of isolationism or mean any kind of axiological relativism. It simply means that should the sufferers and perpetrators of injustice persist in their injustice despite the presentation of the word of God to them, no more could be demanded of the Muslim than to continue to call them to the divine word and to warn human- kind against following their example. The fact that that to which the Muslim calls is through and through moral, obliges him to present his case and have it heard, but not accepted. To accept it freely and deliberately is the moral value the Muslim is seeking. The facts of acceptance and all that follows upon them by way of moral conduct have from his perspective as moral inductor of them only utilitarian, not moral, value. Moral value is that which is involved in the free acceptance of value and acquiescence to its ought-to-do. It should be borne in mind that this restriction applies to the Zionist State which has set up its house on an isolated non-Muslim Island. It does not apply to the Zionist State of Israel, which is guilty of injustice perpetrated against the Jews, the Palestinians and all the Arabs. In her case, the Islamic requirement is jihad, to the end of stopping the ongoing injustice and undoing the injustice committed by it, or on its behalf by the British, since the Balfour Declaration.

F. Islam and the Jewish Problem: The Negative Aspect

What, it may be finally asked, does Islām have to say to the Jewish problem itself, to which Zionism had come as an attempted solution? If Zionism is a false doctrine, and the Zionist state is to be dismantled on account of its injustice, what is to be made of the problem for which Zionism and its state are claimed to be the solution?

1. Failure of Zionism to Provide Security

The first fact to be faced is that Zionism has provided no solution at all to the problem it set itself to solve. The majority of the Jews have not accepted its call to uproot themselves and emigrate to Palestine. An overwhelming majority of them still lives outside Israel and is most likely to continue to do so in the future. New York City alone has more Jews than the whole Zionist State. Although the number of Jewish residents in Europe has been largely reduced by World War II and its aftermath, their numbers are steadily growing again. Neither they, nor their co-religionists in the U.S.S.R. or the Americas are immune from persecution. Indeed, the success of Zionism and the establishment of its state, Israel, have made such persecution nearer, not farther away.

Zionism has cast a frightful question mark on the national loyalty of any Jew around the world. By its insistence that Judaism is a religion, a policy, a race, and a land all in one, Zionism has made it impossible for a Jew to identify himself as a Jew without inviting suspicion from the guardians of the national state of which he is a citizen. The bombastic claim of Zionism in the world press which it largely controls, its posing as the guardian of Jews everywhere, and its acrobatic arrogance in demanding the surrender, and actual commando-like lifting of anti-Jews or anti-Zionists to judge them in its state, are having a world-wide effect of resentment and disgust which may explode one day against the guilty as well as the innocent.

More particularly, in Palestine itself, Zionism has won the deepest enmity of the Palestinians and of all the Arabs and Muslims around them. The latent enmity of the Muslim masses against Zionism and its current protector, the U.S.A., has burst into fury in as far places as Jakarta, Manila and Kuala Lumpur. Despite its internal divisions and other weaknesses, the Arab World and beyond it, the Muslim World, stand bristling with antagonism, awaiting the proper opportunity to pay the Zionists with their own currency. And it is always a question when a change in the international situation will send world Jewry plummeting into another holocaust precisely because of the arrogant use of their power after World War II and the impertinent display of their resentment against humankind.

Zionism has not only contributed to this sad state of affairs. It is directly responsible for it. How, then, can it be said that it had succeeded in providing security for the Jew? Even in the very heartland of Zionism, in Israel, the Jew sits in the mist of an armoury, surrounding himself with barbed wire, minefields and all kinds of weaponry to prevent an onslaught which he knows for certain is coming, sooner or later. His very existence is a regimented spartanism, due in greatest measure to the bounty of international imperialism and colonialism. Thus, Israel, the so-called greatest achievement of Zionism, is really its greatest failure. For the very being of the Zionist state rests, in final analysis, on the passing whim of international politics. Zionism has built its "fortress" on shifting sands.

2. Failure of Zionism to Stop Assimilation

Zionism is supposedly the solution to the problem of assimilation. Assimilation, it must be remembered, was a problem for the Jew living in Christian Europe. The Jews of the rest of Christendom sympathised and many adopted the Zionist view (without opting to emigrate to Palestine) because they felt the problem of the European Jew to be equally their own. To any religiously conscientious Jew, the university campuses of America where the majority of Jewish intelligentsia receive their training is a "disaster area" as far as Judaism is concerned. These Jewish leaders of the future are as secularised as their Christian colleagues. They may be ethnocentrists; but in their minds and hearts there is no faith in God, in revelation, in the absoluteness of the moral law, in man's ultimate responsibility, or in the Day of Judgment. This secularism is so widespread and deep in the Zionist state, excluding the older generation of emigrants from the Muslim World, that the claim that this is the state where Judaism is the be-all and end-all is ridiculously false.

Certainly, it is Zionism which encouraged the spread of such secularism among Jews. It ridiculed the orthodox Jew's faith in a restoration that is eschatological, and hence completely divine in authorship. It repudiated the nature of restoration as being spiritual and taught the restoration of a kingdom in real estate, rocks and gunpowder. It enlandised God by its insistence that the Jew can only be a Jew in Palestine, echoing the enlandising Biblical redactor who, in praising David, asserted that God may be worshipped in and only in David's political capital, Jerusalem (Psalms 132:13-17; II Kings 5:8-

19). Finally, it is Zionism which substituted "ethnic feeling" for the faith in God as source of the ultimate good; and, by its unscrupulous defiant flouting of all moral laws in dealing with those who stood in its way whatever their faith may be, spread cynicism among the Jews of the world.

After the Arabs, the greatest contempt in Israel is reserved for Muslim World Jews who brought with them a remnant of faith in God. It is the clear objective of the Zionist state to Zionise the "oriental Jews"; and this in practice means to "Westernize" them, to cause their thinking to run in Western channels from which God had been banished. Indeed, Zionists are proud that the whole of Israel is a "Western" unit, a "Western" transplant, a "Western" oasis in the Muslim "desert." Western culture, with its basic secularism, cynicism, materialism, and nihilism, constitutes the "*forte*" of the Zionist state.

3. Failure of Zionism to Enable Judaism to Blossom Forth

Has Zionism succeeded in enabling Judaism to recreate itself in thought - philosophy, theology, the sciences; in the arts literature, the visual arts and music; in action-piety and righteousness? The sad truth is that Zionism has not inspired any such attempts. To this day, the world of scholarship knows of no Jewish social sciences, of no Jewish humanities. In the realm of thought, Zionist Jews are tailing the West in all fields. Indeed, Zionist theory itself has been formulated in Hegelian terms. Even in Biblical studies, Zionism has been led by Western scholarship. Nothing is more incongruous than the modern Jewish scholar who makes all sorts of claims for Judaism and Zionism but does so under a Western Christian doctrine of revelation, a Western Christian understanding of the role of his ancestors in *Heilsgeschichte*, or a Hegelian or Marxist interpretation of history.

The same is true of the other domains of thought. The universities and colleges of Israel do not as yet know of a Jewish sociology, a Jewish anthropology, philosophy, political science or economics. All that is being taught and written by Jewish intellectuals stands squarely within the Western tradition.

In the arts, Jewish creativity has been thoroughly Western. Israel, the sovereign state where Jewish genius is to flourish, as yet knows of no music, no dancing, no sculpture, no painting, no architecture that is not Western. What the Jews have brought with them from the Arab countries, from Eastern Europe, the Balkans, North and West Europe, and America is syncretised and labelled "Jewish." The only non-Western element, if any exists at all, is what they have taken from the Arab countries and the Palestinians. But that, because of their hatred of and contempt for everything Arab, is extremely little. When the work of art has a Jewish objective content, like the works of Chagall in painting, or Ernest Bloch in music, it is as little Jewish in form (which after all, according to romanticism, is the definitive aesthetic category!) as Rimsky-Korsakov's Scheherezade and Mozart's II Seraglio are Islamic. Mention needs not be made of the Zionists' circulation in the world of Arab falafel, halāwah, and bread as Israeli foods; of Arab peasant embroidery and couture as Israeli fashions; of Palestinian jewellery and the arts of decoration as Jewish and Israeli handicrafts.

Thus, in the realm of culture, Zionism has been as much a failure as in that of politics. In neither field has it fulfilled its objective. In either case, the reason is that Zionism is at contradiction with itself. In politics, it seeks to save the Jews from persecution by persecuting, from robbery by robbing, from suffering injustice by inflicting injustice. And in culture, it seeks to enable the Jew to be Jewish by Westernising him, by making him a puppet and follower of the West in all fields of human endeavour, from the military to the musical. If the question is pressed further, why would Zionism suffer itself to be in contradiction with itself, the answer is that it itself is nothing, but the romantic disease of the master (the European) passed to the servant-patient (the European Jew). It is of the nature of this European disease to hate that which is not European, especially the Semitic with which Europe has been at war and unsuccessfully-ever since Alexander the Great.

In his Zionist stand, the Zionist is revulsed by all that has revulsed Europe, namely, by everything Semitic. In his sub-conscious mind, possessed by the disease of European romanticism, he hates himself, the Jew, the Semite, the non-European. In the person of the Palestinian, a being who, because of his descendence, traditions, association with the soil of Palestine and the lingering in him of so much of Semitic history, is in every drop the quintessence of Semiticism and Hebrew-ism, the Zionist sees himself as the European romanticist does - at his worst! Aggravating this psychic derangement has been the persistent Western Christian romantic identification of Jesus and the world he lived in as the Palestinian Arab, the Palestinian family, the Palestinian village and countryside, the Palestinian customs of today. As European, the Jew learned and believed this lesson of romantic Christian Europe. The Palestinian Arab was what he wanted as well as hated to be.

G. Islām and the Jewish Problem: The Positive Aspect

If Zionism has proved itself to be such poor solution to the problem of Jewish existence in Christian Europe, what is the alternative? The self-same law of Islam which requires of the Muslim to go to the end of the earth to put an end to injustice must equally apply to the goyim as to the Jewish sufferers of injustice. Can there be any doubt in the Muslim's mind that the Jew is a sufferer of injustice at the hands of the Christian West?

1. The Question of Security

The answer is categorical. Certainly, the Jew has been victim of injustice in the West; and certainly, the Muslim is enjoined by God to come to his rescue, to relieve him from suffering and to help him achieve his freedom, security, and peace. There can therefore be no doubt, Islāmically speaking, that the World of Islām is religiously bound to champion the Jewish cause against Christendom; that it stands indicted as long as it fails to do so. Indeed, championing of the cause of the oppressed has been an essential component of the image of Islam in Makkah and Madinah, in the Muslim World and in Europe. That is why the Jews of Damascus, of Spain, as well as of Constantinople, the Balkans and Central Europe, have helped the Muslims in their conquest of these lands. The Jews themselves were convinced that Islam's and its adherents' championing of justice was genuine. What can Islam offer to the cessation of Jewish suffering in the modern world?

Following World War II and the defeat of Nazism and Fascism, the Jews of the West have made many gains in Europe and the Americas. Today there is no country in Europe and the Americas that does not grant its Jewish citizens the freedom to worship, to work, to elect and be elected to any public office. Equally, there is no country which does not give Israel, the Zionist state, respect far out of proportion to its size and real importance in the world. But since the aims of Zionism have coincided with those of Western imperialism and colonialism, the little state has become enormous by association with the United States and Western Europe. This "enormous" influence, however, is deceiving and, at any rate, temporary. The winds of politics shift suddenly and without evident reason. England, for instance, altered directions radically after 1973; and France, after De Gaulle terminated French colonial- ism in Algeria and composed France's quarrel with the Arab World. In fact, the great influence the Zionist State and Jews in general have wielded since World War II hides behind it a growing resentment and impatience which may break out with the first economic or political crisis.

Moreover, ethnocentrism is still quite dominant in the West, and it is being nourished partly by the forces of romanticism internal to the Western soul, and partly by the success of Zionism, the *non-plus-ultra* cause of ethnic particularism. And yet, the Jews of the West, especially the Zionists, would certainly be the first victims, the first scapegoats and prey, should this ethnocentrism burst out. The other ethnic minorities of the West belong to the servant class and do not constitute a target. Not so the Jews. Masters of the professions, of trade and finance, of communications and the arts, practically everywhere in the Western world, they stand at the forefront of the marked targets.

The Zionists are therefore right in their claim that Jewish security cannot be trusted to Westerners in the long run; that it is only an interval between one wave of anti-Semitism and another in Western history. More important though, is the other claim of

Zionism regarding the future of Jewry in the West; and it is also the truer. That is the claim that wherever and whenever Jewish security is guaranteed in the West, it is certain to result in the dilution of Judaism, the dissipation of Jewish consciousness, and the assimilation of Jews in the Christian world through marriage or culture. It is this danger which is more intractable and insidious, and which prompted many Western Jews to adopt the Zionist cause. The solution of the Jewish problem cannot therefore rest with the guarantee of Western tolerance or the eradication of Western anti-Semiticism. More is certainly needed. It is this "more" that caused Theodor Herzl to find the solution in a sovereign Jewish state. The solution was a tragic mistake though his assessment United States and Western Europe. This "enormous" influence, however, is deceiving and, at any rate, temporary. The winds of politics shift suddenly and without evident reason. England, for instance, altered directions radically after 1973; and France, after De Gaulle terminated French colonialism in Algeria and composed France's quarrel with the Arab World. In fact, the great influence the Zionist State and Jews in general have wielded since World War II hides behind it a growing resentment and impatience which may break out with the first economic or political crisis.

Moreover, ethnocentrism is still quite dominant in the West, and it is being nourished partly by the forces of romanticism internal to the Western soul, and partly by the success of Zionism, the non-plus-ultra cause of ethnic particularism. And yet, the Jews of the West, especially the Zionists, would certainly be the first victims, the first scapegoats and prey, should this ethnocentrism burst out. The other ethnic minorities of the West belong to the servant class and do not constitute a target. Not so the Jews. Masters of the professions, of trade and finance, of communications and the arts practically everywhere in the Western world, they stand at the forefront of the marked targets.

The Zionists are therefore right in their claim that Jewish security cannot be trusted to Westerners in the long run; that it is only an interval between one wave of anti- Semiticism and another in Western history. More important though is the other claim of Zionism regarding the future of Jewry in the West; and it is also the truer. That is the claim that wherever and whenever Jewish security is guaranteed in the West, it is certain to result in the dilution of Judaism, the dissipation of Jewish consciousness, and the assimilation of Jews in the Christian world through marriage or culture. It is this danger which is more intractable and insidious, and which prompted many Western Jews to adopt the Zionist cause. The solution of the Jewish problem cannot therefore rest with the guarantee of Western tolerance or the eradication of Western anti-Semiticism. More is certainly needed. It is this "more" that caused Theodor Herzl to find the solution in a sovereign Jewish state. The solution was a tragic mistake though his assessment of the problem was true.

2. The Right to Immigrate to the Muslim World

Islām offers a perfect solution to the Jewish problem, which has beset the Jews and the West for two millennia. This solution is for the Jews of the world to be given the right to dwell wherever they wish, as free citizens of the state of their choice. Those who feel themselves reasonably happy where they are and wish to continue to live there ought to be entitled by a world-covenant to do so. As to those Jews who desire to emigrate from the West, they ought to be welcome in the Muslim World. If, for reasons of religious attachment, they wish to live in those areas of the Muslim World associated with their history - Egypt to Mesopotamia - they ought to be entitled to do so by virtue of the respect Islām pays to the Prophets of God and the necessary extension of sympathy and love for those that honour the prophetic tradition and the spaces in which it conveyed its divine messages.

On this question of Jewish immigration Islām gives far more to world Jewry than Zionism. The latter wants only Palestine; Islam forces wide open the gates of the whole Muslim World, and a fortiori, of the Arab World; and still more, of the territory of the "Fertile Crescent." "Immigration" however does not mean seizure of land, displacement, or dispossession of others. Neither does it mean seizure of the state, or its transformation into a state for the Jews on the German or French model. Ex hypothesi, there must be an Islamic state comprehending these territories; an Islamic state whose constitution is the Qur'an, whose law is the Shari'ah, and whose constituency is only partly non-Muslim. Such Islamic state extending from the Atlantic to the Malay Basin, is certainly obliged to open its gates to any Jewish immigrant who travels thither. Such an Islamic state is the haven for world Jewry, as well as the protector and defender of prophecy and its peoples against all outside attack. Such a state is a world state, with infinite geo-political depth, infinite geographic and human resources. Endowed with the life- and world-affirming ideology that Islam is, and with a long history of confrontation with the world, and the richest culture and civilization, such an Islamic state can effectively contend on the world scene and has the capacity requisite therefor.

Contrasted with such an Islamic state, the state of Israel which Zionism presents is a miserable match. It consists of a few thousand square kilometres, a sliver of land, and three million people. True, it is at present armed to the teeth with the most up-to-date and sophisticated weaponry. But it depends for its military muscle as well as the very food it consumes on Western Imperialism whose direction may change from moment to moment. Moreover, it is surrounded with a wall of resentment and hatred in the will of a hundred and fifty million Arabs and a billion Muslims, awaiting the shift in international relations which would give them occasion to pounce on it.

If world Jewry, or a substantial number of its members, or, if only the present Jewish citizens of Israel were to exist in an Islamic state, how might they live in accordance with Judaism? How may Jewish genius be given the chance to prosper and flower forth?

3. The Right to Peace

The first requisite for any culture, civilisation, or religion to prosper - which is the same for any community to do so - is peace. The reassurance that one is safe as to life and property is absolutely necessary for the mind to operate in any long-term or constructive manner. Without it, no human can develop the taste or the will for truth, goodness, or beauty. True, Nietzsche and von Treitschke have a point that war and danger do cultivate discipline as well as idealism. But no less true is the fact that they never sustain either value for any long time. Sparta, Imperialist Japan and Nazi Germany have not been able to do it despite the tremendously more favourable conditions they possessed by comparison with Zionist Israel. Such lasting peace cannot be assured to the Jews anywhere except by Islām and under its political dominion. The relation of Islām to Judaism being one of sympathy, nay of identity, Islam's religious honouring of the Hebrew prophets as God's prophets and of the Hebrew revelation as God's revelation furnishes the best guarantee. Here is a nation, an ummah of a billion souls on the march maintaining this faith as essential and constitutive element of its own religion, of its own consciousness of God, of itself and of the world. As with Muhammad (*sallä Allahu 'alayhi wa sallam*) and his companions, the ummah of Islām firmly believes that God is the Guardian of the Jews and other non-Muslims who opt for peace rather than war with the Islamic State. Indeed, in the faith and law of Islam, the guaran- tee is provided even against corrupt Muslim rulers who might be tempted to exploit or aggress upon the dhimmis, or covenanters who covenanted for peace under God's guarantee ship. Finally, there is the guarantee of tested history. Except for the briefest intervals in which Muslims have suffered even more than Jews or Christians at the hands of a corrupt ruler, the history of Islam's tolerance and coexistence with Judaism and Christianity is pure white. Throughout the fourteen centuries of its existence, its record is without blemish. Never has the ummah conceived of itself or of its mission, of its past or of its future, as involving a necessary decimation of the non- Muslims living in its midst.

The guarantee which Islām offers to the Jews is the best; for it is eternal as well as the most efficient. Whatever may be written in a constitution may be amended since the nation's will, a majority of 51 or 66 per cent, have voted it as such and can as well vote its contrary. But when the law is God's writing and ordinance, it cannot ever be changed. Even national culture has modes and fashions and may change; not religion, which forms the very conscience of the overwhelming majority of the billion Muslims.

4. The Right to Self-Determination by the Torah

Before leaving the question of Jewish security under Islām, one more problem remains. Is it not necessary for the feeling of peace that the Jews enjoy national sovereignty like the European countries do? No! The feeling for national sovereignty is a very recent development, even in the West. It is an outgrowth of ethnocentrism and political nationalism and the offspring of European romanticism in the last two centuries. The European has existed and prospered for centuries without it. Loyalty to God, to the Church, to the universal community, to king and prince, does not require it. "National sovereignty," as the third constitutive element of the state after "people" and "a piece of earth with defined borders," is itself a part of the disease of romanticism. "Sovereignty" is a vague and woozy concept, supposed to weld "people" and "earth" into mystical unity precisely in order to exclude all other elements. When it was first called for in Europe, it was meant to exclude the jurisdiction of the Church in affairs of the community. Later, as the Church influence withered, it was meant to exclude Christian ethics and values from determining public affairs. It is neither needed nor called for by the nationalists when the matter is one of determining human lives in the conduct of concrete daily life. Its function is to nourish the mystique of nation as Fustel de Coulanges had conceived of it in the last century.

And yet, it is here, in the very domain of concrete daily living, that sovereignty is necessary. Islam grants it to the Jews as well as to other non-Muslims without reservations. Here, it means the authority of the Torah to guide concrete action, the Jew's freedom to observe the Law of God. The Western national state denies it to its Jewish citizens despite all assurances of the right to life, property and the pursuit of happiness the constitution may have granted equally to all citizens.

In the domain of concrete personal living, Islām unquestionably yields all authority to the non-Muslims to determine their lives as they alone see fit. It not only permits, but requires them, to live in accordance with their own laws. To this purpose it regards them as an ummah, different and separate from the Muslims and all non-Jews, endowed with traditions and institutions. It requires the Jews to set up their own rabbinic courts and puts its whole executive power at their disposal. The Shari'ah, the law of Islām, demands of all Jews to submit themselves to the precepts of Jewish law as interpreted by the rabbinic courts, and treats any defiance or contempt of the rabbinic court as rebellion against the Islamic state itself, on a par with like action on the part of any Muslim vis-à-vis the Islamic court.

Moreover, the whole ethic and culture of the state, the country and the population, stress the value of religion, of piety and the ways of God, of righteousness and moral action, of the ummah - society and community - as the consensus of mind (vision), of heart (judgment) and of arm (action) in the service of God, as the universal brotherhood under the moral law. Such an atmosphere is precisely what is required to promote the Jew's feeling for and commitment to Jewishness, to the revelation of Moses and the covenant of Abraham. The atmosphere provided by Islām is so favourable, and that provided by the secularist Christian West is so antagonistic to Judaism that the religion of Moses seems destined to flower under Islam's dominion, in cooperation and co-existence with the Muslims, or dissolve itself in secular Western culture.

Where the matter concerns a single Jew or more persons of Jewish faith, that matter is definitely to be disposed of by the Jewish rabbinic court alone, influenced by its own understanding of the Torah, of the Halakah and of the Jewish tradition. Whatever its judgment, the Muslims and the Islamic state are bound by law to acquiesce to it, and to attend to its execution as long as dominion and executive power is in their hands. Where a matter concerns two adherents, one of whom is a Jew and the other a non-Jew, Islām requires that each be treated according to his own law. Where the dispositions of the two laws are at variance with each other, Islām requires the state to interfere and compose the difference. Such composition by the state may not be arbitrary or capricious. It must be based on the principle of Maslahah or benefit, of the parties concerned first, and the two ummahs behind them. This principle is so pervasive in Islamic jurisprudence that it can serve as legitimate base for composing the gravest differences. Even murder, under Islamic law, is compensable. The mediating judgment is always subject to appeal to the higher court. Above the highest court stands the law of God which is open to the inspection of and invocation by anybody against any authority, including that of the caliph himself.

5. Defence of the Islamic State

The only area removed from the *dhimmi* community's jurisdiction is that of war and peace. This is the exclusive domain of the Islamic state whose raison d'être is the establishment of peace and the critical presentation of the word of God. This duty is that of defence of Dar al Islam - that is, the ummah of Muslims as well as those of the non-Muslims who have entered the *Pax Islâmica*. Since the Islamic state is really a federation of community-states, it is only right and befitting that no community-state be held responsible for the conduct of foreign policy, of peace and war, and that the federal state be so. Two major differences exist between a federal state, such as the Islamic state, and one like the United States or Switzerland. The first is that in the latter, the constituent is a mini-state based on territory, whereas in the former, it is based on humans in community, thus giving primacy to the humans rather than to real estate. The second is that the law of the Western federal state is positive in the sense that it is what the majority of the constituents (whatever its percentage) decide it to be at any time; whereas the law of the Islamic state is what God has ordained for it for all time.

H. The Islamic Solution and the Status Quo in the Arab World

Finally, it may be asked, how would the application of the Islamic solution affect the actual state of affairs in the Near East?

First, the Arab states of the Near East must undergo a transformation from being caricatures of the Western national states to becoming a single, united Islamic state. The Arab states are literally all creations of Western colonialism. They must all be dismantled, and their populations reorganized into the Islamic state. Their laws which again for the most part they had inherited from Western colonialism ought to be discarded in favour of the Shari'ah, or law of Islam. The Islamic state emerging from their union should abolish all frontiers between them, all their individual defence establishments, and assume all responsibility for defence and foreign affairs. Only if this is achieved may the Arab Muslims of the Near East stand ready to implement the Islamic solution of the problem of Israel.

Second, Israel, the Zionist state, would be dismantled, by force, if necessary. The institution of the Zionist state is a positive evil, and so is all its defence establishment. This leaves the ummah of Jews as covenanter with the Islamic state for peace. The Jewish citizens of Israel would not be required to move. On the contrary, they would be invited to dwell in any city or village of the whole Islamic state, not only in some pieces of real estate on the West Bank of the Jordan and in the Gaza strip as Zionism is presently asking. But no Jew may dispossess a Muslim of his land, house or other property as Zionists have so far done. The transaction is personal; and both parties, buyer, and seller, have to will the sale and be satisfied with it. As for the Palestinians, they would have to be rehabilitated in their own homes and lands, out of which they had been forcefully ejected first by British and then by Zionist arms. Moreover, they would have to be compensated, under Islamic law, for their damages.

This means that the Jews presently living in stolen homes and cultivating stolen lands, will have either to vacate or to compensate their owners. If the owners insist on evacuation, the capital necessary for compensation could be used to buy new land and home elsewhere. If, as Jews claim, the Kingdom of David extended from the River of Egypt to the Euphrates, there is still plenty of land for them to purchase and occupy. According to Islam, as it has been already said, there is no restriction whatever on the number of Jewish immigrants, nor on the area or locality of land they may purchase to dwell in throughout the Muslim World.

Thirdly, once the bouleversement this solution brings has settled down, there is no reason why the Jews, as Dhimmī citizens of the Islamic state, may not keep all the public institutions they have so far developed in Palestine (Courts of law, learned societies of art and culture, public corporations, schools, colleges and universities) to continue in their operation, whether in any locality of Palestine or anywhere else where Jews might choose to dwell. Henceforth, their vision and their efforts would be directed toward upholding and promoting Judaism, not the Western ideologies of decadence and aberration. No one will make war against them. No one will persecute or molest them. Their task is to be as Jewish as they care to be.

Then, when the Jews of the emerging Islamic state have organised themselves and began to breathe as Jews, free from any threat, the chief of the Islamic state might repeat the message which an earlier predecessor of his (Muhammad, "the second," conqueror of Constantinople) had sent to the chief of an earlier non-Muslim ummah in the Islamic state (Gennadius Scholarius, Patriarch of Constantinople): "Be the Patriarch of your ummah in peace. May Allah protect you. To you, our friendship is pledged in all circumstances and under all conditions, wherever it may benefit you. May you enjoy all the privileges hitherto enjoyed by your predecessors!" (G. Papadopoulos, *Les privilèges du patriarchat oecumeniques (Communauté grecque-orthodoxe) dans l'empire ottoman*, Paris, 1924, p. 10).